EMPOWERING TOMORROW'S LEADERS

A Guide for Teens

By

Sumit Sharma

MBA, MBB, SCPM, CHFP, ACHE

Published by Sharmx LLC
Disclaimer

This book is intended to provide general information and practical guidance on leadership and personal development for teenagers. The advice, examples, and case studies included in this book are based on the author's personal experiences and research; however, the information is not intended as a substitute for professional advice in educational, psychological, or legal matters.

The author and publisher make no representations or warranties regarding the accuracy, applicability, or completeness of the contents of this book. Any action you take based on the information presented is at your own risk, and the author and publisher disclaim all liability for any direct, indirect, incidental, or consequential damages arising from the use of this material.

The stories, case studies, and examples are included for illustrative purposes only. Any resemblance to real persons, living or dead, is purely coincidental unless explicitly stated. The author and publisher do not guarantee specific outcomes and disclaim responsibility for how readers interpret or implement the material. Readers are encouraged to seek mentorship, professional advice, and guidance for specific concerns.

The trademarks, brand names, and organizations mentioned in this book are used for reference purposes only and are the property of their respective owners. Their inclusion does not imply endorsement or affiliation.

Legal Jurisdiction: This publication is governed by the laws of the United States. Any disputes arising from this publication shall be subject to the exclusive jurisdiction of the relevant courts in the U.S.

ISBN: 979-8-9922910-4-9

Table of Contents

Acknowledgments iii

Introduction: *Discovering The Leader Within* iv

A Note From The Author xix

Chapter 1: The Power Of Leadership 1

Chapter 2: The Fear Of Speaking And How To Overcome It 21

Chapter 3: The Basics Of Debate 49

Chapter 4: Design Thinking For Problem-Solving 74

Chapter 5: Building Emotional Intelligence 104

Chapter 6: Goal Setting And Time Management 129

Chapter 7: Self-Discipline Building The Habits That Shape Your Future 152

Chapter 8: Emotional Intelligence Understanding Yourself And Others 163

Chapter 9: Resilience – Bouncing Back From Setbacks 180

Chapter 10: Vision – Seeing The Big Picture And Setting Goals For The Future 185

Chapter 11: Leadership In The Age Of Ai And Beyond 190

Chapter 12: Key Takeaways And Next Steps 214

Supplementary Materials: Tools To Empower Your Leadership Journey 219

Closing Note 223

About The Author 225

Acknowledgments

This book is dedicated to the people who have been my guiding stars, my greatest supporters, and my source of endless inspiration.

To my incredible parents, Prof. Dr. Meena Sharma and Mr. V. N. Sharma, for shaping me with values of resilience, empathy, and service. Your unwavering love and wisdom have been the foundation of my life.

To my wonderful wife, Deepti Sharma, my true north, whose unwavering support and sacrifices have made this book possible. Your belief in me and your patience have given me the space and strength to pursue my passion.

To my amazing children, Savar, Vyom, and Saesha, whose curiosity, dreams, and ambitions inspire me every day. You are the reason I wrote this book, and you remind me that the future is always worth building.

To my brother, Varun Sharma, and my sister, Dr. Bulbul Salwan, for your constant encouragement, wisdom, and belief in me. Your presence in my life has always been a source of comfort and strength.

And finally, to everyone who has taught me something along the way—mentors, colleagues, students, and friends—thank you for the lessons, the challenges, and the inspiration. Your stories and your support have shaped the leader I am today.

This book is a reflection of all the people who have walked with me on this journey. I am deeply grateful to each of you.

Introduction

Discovering The Leader Within

Emma sat alone at her lunch table, staring at the rows of students absorbed in their phones. The cafeteria felt more like a waiting room than a place to connect. A year of remote learning had made face-to-face conversations awkward and distant. The buzz of laughter and chatter that used to fill the space had been replaced by silence, interrupted only by the hum of vending machines.

Emma wasn't the person people called "a natural leader." She didn't dominate class discussions or run for student council. She was just observant. What she noticed was this: no one was talking, but everyone seemed to wish someone would.

It wasn't some grand plan at first. She didn't set out to change school. She just thought, *what if lunch didn't have to feel this lonely?* That simple thought sparked a new question: *What if I did something about it?*

The next day, Emma pulled a stack of sticky notes from her backpack and wrote:

"Connection Corner: Join us in Room 202. Stories, laughs, and snacks."

She didn't overthink it. She didn't ask for permission. She just put the notes on lockers, hoping at least a few people would appear. When lunch came, her heart raced as she walked to Room 202, half expecting to sit alone.

But there they were—two first-year students she didn't know well, standing awkwardly by the door. Emma smiled and waved them in.

Small Moments, Big Ripples

By the end of the week, Connection Corner had ten regulars. They weren't the loudest or most popular students. They were the quiet ones, like Emma, who wanted something more. They played trivia games and shared funny stories from childhood. The following week, someone brought homemade cookies. Two weeks later, the room was packed, and people had stopped staring at their phones. Emma's school wasn't perfect—but it felt more connected.

That's the thing about leadership—it often starts in quiet moments. It doesn't always begin with speeches or titles. Sometimes, it's a simple question: *What if I tried?*

The Myth of "Natural Leaders"

Many people believe you're born with leadership—a gift reserved for the charismatic, the bold, or the loud. But here's the truth: leadership isn't about being born special. It's about seeing something that could be better and deciding to do something about it.

In sports, teammates might stay late to help others practice. In your family, the sibling might step up when things get tough. At school, it might be the person who notices someone sitting alone and invites them over. These moments might not seem "heroic" at first glance, but they are.

The leaders who change the world are usually the ones who start small—just like Emma.

Your First Leadership Moment

Remember when you noticed something that could have been better—maybe a classmate struggling, a project needing direction, or a disorganized event? Did you feel that tug? Is that little voice asking you to step in?

Leadership starts there, with that feeling. The difference between leaders and bystanders is what happens next. Do you silence that voice, thinking someone else will handle it? Or do you listen and act?

You don't need anyone's permission to lead. You don't need a title. All you need is the courage to ask, *What if?*

Why Leadership Matters for Teens

The world doesn't wait for leaders to show up. Often, leaders emerge because they see something others don't. They see a possibility where others know the routine. But for teenagers, leadership doesn't always seem urgent—after all, isn't that something for adults?

The truth is the teenage years are when the seeds of leadership are planted. What you choose to do now—in small or significant ways—can ripple into your future and the futures of people you haven't yet met.

The Story of Arjun: A Simple Idea, a Lasting Impact

Arjun's high school wasn't known for innovation. The same clubs met year after year, and students followed the same path: class, homework, repeat. But Arjun noticed a gap. While the school prided itself on academics, it had no mentorship program to help first-year students adjust to the pressures of high school.

Arjun didn't have all the answers, but he had a vision—a program where older students helped younger ones navigate everything from classes to friendship struggles. He recruited three friends, wrote a proposal, and pitched it to the principal. After some hesitation, the school gave him a shot.

By his senior year, the mentorship program had expanded to over 40 student mentors. The dropout rate for incoming first-year students decreased, and new students felt a stronger sense of belonging. Arjun didn't set out to change the school's culture—he just saw a need and acted on it.

This is why leadership matters. It's not about prestige—it's about presence. It's about being present enough to notice what others overlook and bold enough to believe you can improve it.

Why Now?

Some people think *I'll lead when I'm older*. But leadership doesn't have an age requirement. If anything, the earlier you start, the more you learn and grow. The teenage years are like a laboratory for leadership—full of experiments, failures, and breakthroughs. The habits you form now—how you handle challenges, work with others, and respond to setbacks—shape the leader you'll become.

When you think about leaders you admire—activists, athletes, scientists, or creators—ask yourself, *What were they like at my age?* Most of them didn't have it all figured out. But they had curiosity, courage, and a willingness to grow.

A Changing World, a Growing Need

The world you're growing up in is changing faster than any generation before. Social media, artificial intelligence, and climate change aren't distant topics in textbooks. They're shaping your reality right now. With these changes come both uncertainty and opportunity.

Leaders in this era aren't just those who know the most—they're the ones who can adapt, collaborate, and inspire others. The future belongs to those who can turn information into action, ideas into solutions, and setbacks into comebacks.

The Legacy of Teen Leaders

History is filled with stories of young leaders who changed the world long before they became adults. Malala Yousafzai stood up for girls' education at 15. Greta Thunberg launched a global climate movement at 16. These teenagers didn't wait for someone to tell them they could lead. They started by standing up for their beliefs and inspiring others to follow.

But leadership isn't just about global change—it's about your everyday impact. The classmate you helped study for a math test. The community drive you volunteered for. The kindness you showed when no one else noticed. Leadership happens in these quiet moments too.

A Personal Challenge

Think of one thing in your school, home, or community that could be better. Maybe your school's clubs are outdated, or new students struggle to feel welcome. Maybe your community doesn't have enough volunteer initiatives that matter to you. Instead of asking yourself why things are the way they are, ask yourself: *Why not me?*

You don't have to wait to be ready. You just have to be willing.

The world is looking for leaders—not someday, but now. And you have everything you need to start.

The Challenges and Opportunities of Leadership

Leadership is often described as a journey, but people rarely talk about the roadblocks along the way. They paint a picture of celebrated and admired leaders standing on podiums. They don't show the moments of doubt, failure, and loneliness that come with leading.

What makes leadership both challenging and rewarding is that it's not a straight path—it's full of unexpected twists, setbacks, and moments when you feel like giving up. But it's also filled with breakthroughs, surprising victories, and connections you never imagined. The challenges of leadership are real, but so are the opportunities.

The Hard Truth About Leading

Aria wasn't driven by popularity when she decided to run for class president. She wanted to advocate for mental health programs at her school after seeing her best friend struggle in silence. She spent weeks crafting her campaign speech, staying after school to meet with teachers, and building a team of students who believed in her vision.

Aria stood before her classmates on election day and poured her heart into her speech. But when the results came in, she lost. Her classmates chose someone else—the student with more friends, not necessarily more ideas.

Aria felt crushed. She questioned whether she was meant to be a leader at all. But instead of disappearing into the background, she asked herself a different question, *What can I do, even without a title?*

That question changed everything. Instead of walking away, Aria decided to start a mental health club that didn't need approval or an election to make an impact. By the end of the school year, her club had organized mental health awareness workshops, built a peer support network, and convinced the school to bring in a counselor for student drop-ins.

Aria's story shows that leadership isn't always rewarded as expected. You might not get the title. You might not get applause. However, true leaders focus on the impact, not the credit.

When Things Don't Go as Planned
Failure is one of the most complex parts of leadership, but it's also one of the most outstanding teachers. Every leader, from Nobel Prize winners to entrepreneurs, has faced failure. The difference is how they respond to it.

Do they walk away? Or do they learn from it, adjust their approach, and keep going?

One of the biggest challenges young leaders face is fear of looking foolish, rejection, and failing in front of others. But here's the truth: failing doesn't make you weak. Failing and getting back up makes you stronger than you ever thought possible.

In the 1990s, NASA engineer Diana Trujillo immigrated from Colombia with almost no English skills and barely enough money for a plane ticket. After countless setbacks—failing exams and struggling to pay for school—she eventually led a team that helped land the Mars Rover. When asked what kept her going, she said, *"Every failure taught me that I was stronger than my doubts."*

Failure doesn't end your leadership—it fuels it.

The Opportunities Within Challenges

Every challenge is an opportunity in disguise. When you face resistance, it means you're doing something meaningful. When you make mistakes, it means you're learning. The most innovative leaders—whether they're activists, scientists, or athletes—didn't succeed by avoiding failure. They succeeded by growing from it.

As a teenager, you're in one of life's most exciting and challenging phases. The world is constantly changing, and you're expected to figure out who you are and where you fit in. But this phase also gives you something that most adults lose: the freedom to experiment, dream big, and take risks.

Leadership isn't about avoiding difficulties—it's about facing them head-on and knowing that every setback is a step toward something more significant.

Your Leadership Mindset

When you encounter obstacles—losing an election, failing a test, or facing rejection—remind yourself: this isn't the end. It's part of your story. The most inspiring leaders are the ones who keep going when things are tough.

Here's a question to carry with you: *What will I learn from this challenge?* Asking this doesn't make the challenge more manageable but gives it meaning. And when you find meaning in difficult moments, you grow.

Leadership will challenge and change you in ways that make every setback worth it.

What This Book Offers

Picture this: You're standing at the starting line of a long journey. You don't have a map, just an idea of where you want to go. The path is unknown and filled with challenges, choices, and surprises. Now imagine someone hands you a guide—not a book that tells you every step you should take, but one that helps you discover your strengths, sharpen your instincts, and prepare for the unexpected.

That's what this book is. It's not a rulebook or a manual. It's a toolkit filled with stories, lessons, and practical exercises to help you grow as a leader, no matter where you start.

Blueprint for Action

This book isn't about impressive theories that don't apply to real life. It's about action—what you can do today, tomorrow, and next week to become a leader who makes a lasting impact. Each chapter builds on the last, giving you new insights and challenges to push you out of your comfort zone.

You'll learn how to:

❖ *Speak confidently in front of any audience, whether two people or 200.*
❖ *Turn ideas into solutions using creative problem-solving frameworks.*
❖ *Collaborate with peers who may not always agree with you— and still achieve incredible results.*
❖ *Manage your time like a pro, balancing school, sports, family, and personal goals.*

But more importantly, this book will help you understand *why* leadership matters and how you can make a difference, even when the odds are stacked against you.

Real Stories, Real Lessons

Every chapter includes stories of teenagers like you— students who took the initiative, failed, succeeded, and grew. You'll read about Priya, who turned her love for science into an after-school mentorship program that inspired dozens of younger students. You'll meet Noah, who turned a community garden project into a movement for sustainable living in his neighborhood.

These aren't superheroes or characters from movies—they're real people who started where you are now. They didn't wait for someone to permit them to lead. They saw an opportunity, took a leap, and learned.

Your Leadership Toolbox

Leadership isn't just about making speeches or organizing events—it's about mastering small, everyday habits that make you stronger. This book is complete of practical exercises designed to help you sharpen your skills:

- ❖ *Exercises to help you find your voice and tell your story.*
- ❖ *Brainstorming activities to teach you how to approach problems from different angles.*
- ❖ *Group challenges to build your teamwork and conflict resolution abilities.*

Each exercise is meant to challenge you—not with impossible tasks, but with small steps that build your confidence and expand your abilities over time.

A Personal Guide, Not Just a Book

This book isn't just something you read once and forget. It's meant to grow with you. The lessons apply whether you're working on a class project, leading a sports team, or organizing a community event. As you take on more significant challenges, you'll find that the skills you develop become second nature.

Leadership is a journey; you need to pack essentials like any other. Like any journey you took, this is part of your leadership backpack—a resource you can return to whenever you need direction, motivation, or a reminder of why you started.

The goal isn't for you to follow a formula but to create your own path.

Journey Starts Here

By the end of this book, you won't just know *what* leadership is—you'll know how it feels to lead. You'll have the tools to build meaningful connections, navigate challenges, and inspire change. More importantly, you'll be confident to step forward, even when the way isn't clear.

The chapters ahead are designed to meet you where you are and help you grow. Whether you're already leading in your school or just starting to find your voice, this book is your companion for the journey ahead.

The only thing left to do is take that first step.

A Journey of Growth

Leadership isn't a destination; it's a process filled with victories, setbacks, and moments of self-discovery. The version of you that starts this book won't be the same version as the one who finishes it. Leadership will change you.

But here's the truth: that most people don't talk. Discussion isn't always easy. It's uncomfortable. It means learning to stretch yourself, facing your weaknesses, and embracing the times when things don't go as planned. But that's where fundamental transformation happens—not in the moments when everything feels easy, but in the moments when you push forward despite the uncertainty.

The Story of Lucas: From Self-Doubt to Strength

Lucas was the kind of kid who always stayed in the background. In group projects, he let others take the lead. He was thoughtful and creative, but he doubted himself. He was afraid of messing up, of making the wrong decision in front of others.

Then, in his junior year, something unexpected happened. His history teacher asked him to lead a class debate on climate change. Lucas froze. He wanted to say no. But before he could, his teacher said something stuck: "Leadership isn't about knowing all the answers—it's about having the courage to start the conversation."

Lucas didn't sleep the night before the debate. He researched until his eyes blurred, rehearsed his points in front of his mirror, and braced himself for failure. But when the discussion began, something shifted. He spoke clearly and with purpose. His classmates leaned in, not because he was perfect, but because he was honest.

By the time the bell rang, Lucas knew he wasn't the same person who had walked into that room. That debate wasn't just about climate change but about changing how he saw himself.

The Uncomfortable Truth About Growth

Growth can feel awkward. You'll make mistakes. You'll second-guess yourself. And sometimes, you'll want to quit. But these moments are proof that you're stepping outside your comfort zone.

Imagine planting a seed. For that seed to grow into something substantial—a tree or a flower—it has to break through the soil. Growth is messy before it's beautiful. And leadership is the same.

As a teenager, you're at a time in your life when you're expected to figure out who you are, navigate social circles, excel academically, and prepare for the future—all at once. It's a lot. But it's also a chance to grow in ways that will shape you forever.

Learning from Every Step

Every leader you admire has gone through seasons of uncertainty. They've faced failure, fear, and self-doubt. The difference is that they didn't let those moments define them—they let those moments refine them.

Michael Jordan didn't make his high school varsity basketball team at first. Twelve publishers rejected J.K. Rowling before *Harry Potter* became a phenomenon. These leaders share a willingness to grow, even when the odds seem stacked against them.

You will have moments of wondering if you're cut out to lead. That's normal. What matters is what you do next. Will you give up, or will you try again? Will you see setbacks as proof that you're not good enough or as signs that you're on the brink of something new?

Becoming the Best Version of You

The journey of leadership isn't about becoming someone else—it's about becoming more of who you already are. You don't need to imitate your school's loudest or most popular people. You don't need to pretend to be fearless or flawless.

True leaders are those who embrace their quirks, learn from their flaws, and lead with authenticity. They know that growth doesn't happen overnight—it's built through daily choices: choosing to speak up even when it's scary, listening when others need a voice, and believing in yourself when doubt creeps in.

A Challenge for the Road Ahead

As you read this book, you'll encounter lessons that challenge you. Some will make you reflect. Others will push you to act. But every challenge is meant to help you grow into the kind of leader you've always had the potential to become.

Leadership isn't a solo journey—it's filled with moments where you'll connect with others, seek advice, and mentor those who come after you. Growth isn't linear. Some days, you'll feel unstoppable. On other days, you'll feel like you're back at square one. And that's okay.

The important thing is to keep going. Every small step brings you closer to the leader you're meant to be.

A Note From The Author

When I was your age, I didn't think of myself as a leader. Like many teenagers, I believed leadership was reserved for adults— CEOs in boardrooms, politicians at podiums, and coaches on the sidelines. Leaders were the people on stage, making speeches or leading crowds. I never thought leadership could apply to someone like me.

But life has a way of surprising you. I learned that leadership isn't about the spotlight but your choices when no one's watching. It's about how you treat people, show up, and handle the moments when things don't go your way.

I didn't feel ready the first time I took a leadership role. I was asked to lead a small team while still figuring things out myself. I felt overwhelmed, full of self-doubt, and convinced I would mess up. And I messed up—plenty of times. But what I learned was that mistakes are part of the process.

I've since had the chance to lead in ways I never expected— whether in the corporate world, volunteer work, or mentoring others. But the lessons I've learned all come back to the same truth: leadership is less about perfection and more about persistence. It's less about telling people what to do and more about inspiring them to see what's possible.

I wrote this book because I believe the world needs more young leaders. Your generation is stepping into a world filled with incredible challenges and opportunities. You're growing up in a time when technology is advancing faster than we can keep up, where global problems like climate change, inequality, and mental health crises are shaping daily life. But with those challenges come new chances to lead.

This book isn't just a guide—it's a conversation. It's a way for me to share the lessons I've learned so that you can apply them in your life. I don't expect you to agree with everything in these pages. I hope you challenge yourself to think critically and form your leadership philosophy.

Throughout this book, you'll read stories of teens who stepped up in moments big and small. Some of them changed their schools. Some changed their communities. And some changed their own lives in ways they never thought possible. I hope their stories will remind you that leadership doesn't come from waiting for the perfect moment but from deciding that *now* is the right time to act.

By the time you finish this book, I hope you see yourself not just as someone who could be a leader someday but as someone who can lead right now. I'm rooting for you and can't wait to see what you'll accomplish.

CHAPTER 1

THE POWER OF LEADERSHIP

When you hear the word "leader," what comes to mind? A president giving a speech to a packed auditorium? A coach motivating their team before the big game? Maybe you picture someone with authority—a captain, a CEO, or a teacher before the class.

But what if I told you that leadership has nothing to do withstanding in the spotlight and everything to do with the small, quiet choices you make every day? What if I told you that some of the most outstanding leaders in history were once just like you—trying to figure out where they fit in, second-guessing themselves, unsure of their path?

The Story of Emily: A Small Act of Courage

Let me tell you about Emily. She wasn't someone most people noticed in high school. She sat in the middle row of the class, wasn't the first to raise her hand, and kept her friends' circle small. Something about her that stood out was her sense of empathy. She noticed when people felt left out, even if she didn't always know what to do about it.

One rainy Monday morning, Emily noticed her classmate James sitting alone at lunch. James had recently transferred from another state, and his body language spoke louder than words— hunched shoulders, eyes fixed on his sandwich, headphones in to block out the world. Emily felt a pull, a voice in her head that whispered, *Say something. Just invite him over.*

But then doubt crept in. *What if he thinks I'm weird? What if my friends do?*

She could've walked away. Instead, she approached and said, "Hey, there's space at our table. Come sit with us."

It was just one small gesture to Emily—an invitation that took ten seconds. But to James, it was everything. He later admitted that he'd been feeling invisible, wondering if he'd ever fit in at this new school. That single act of kindness shifted his entire experience.

That's the power of leadership. It's not always about grand speeches or big decisions—it's about choosing courage in the small moments, even when it's uncomfortable.

The Myth of the "Born Leader"

One of the biggest misconceptions about leadership is that you have to be born with some unique "leader gene." People assume that the best leaders are the loudest, the boldest, or the most popular. But the truth? Leadership isn't something you're born with—it's something you practice.

Michael Jordan, one of the greatest athletes ever, wasn't born a leader. He was cut from his high school basketball team before he became the superstar everyone knows. Oprah Winfrey wasn't born with millions of viewers—she was told she wasn't fit for television before becoming one of the world's most influential leaders.

The leaders you admire didn't start as icons. They became leaders because they failed, learned, and kept showing up.

Why Some People Step Up and Others Don't

Have you ever noticed how, when things get hard, some people jump into action while others shrink back? Why is that? Psychologists say it concerns a person's locus of control.

Internal Locus of Control: People who believe they control their actions and outcomes. They think that their choices matter.

External Locus of Control: People who believe life just happens to them—that success or failure is determined by luck, fate, or what other people do.

Teenagers who believe in their ability to shape their lives are likelier to take initiative. And here's the good news: this isn't fixed. You can train your mind to shift from thinking, *This isn't in my control. What's* one *thing I can do to improve this?*

Every leader starts with a single choice: taking responsibility instead of waiting for someone else.

Finding Your "Why"

The strongest leaders—the ones who inspire others and create lasting change—are the ones who know their "why." This isn't some vague sense of wanting to "be successful" or "make a difference." Your "why" is the deeply personal reason that drives you to step up, even when it's hard.

Think about someone you admire—maybe a teacher, a coach, or a family member. Why do you respect them? Chances are it's not just because they're good at what they do. It's because you see how much they care. Their "why" shines through in their actions.

As a teenager, you're in the perfect stage of life to start discovering your "why." What gets you fired up? What problems do you care about solving? It could be bullying, climate change, mental health, or making your school more inclusive. Your "why" doesn't have to be perfect—it just has to be meaningful to you.

A Leadership Moment of Your Own

The first step to becoming a leader is recognizing that you already have opportunities to lead. You practice leadership whenever you stand up for someone, contribute an idea, or help solve a problem.

Emily doesn't think she is doing anything extraordinary when she invites James to her table. But her small act of courage planted the seed for something bigger—a sense of belonging that rippled outward.

Your leadership moment might not look like a scene from a movie. It might be as simple as starting a conversation, raising your hand, or volunteering to lead a group project. But that moment, no matter how small, is what builds the foundation of the leader you're becoming.

Your Turn

Ask yourself: What's one small thing you can do today to improve someone else's day? It doesn't have to be groundbreaking—it just has to be authentic. Write it down, and the next time that tiny voice in your head says, *Maybe I should...* listen to it.

Because that's how leaders are made—one decision at a time.

Defining Leadership Beyond Titles

Leadership is often misunderstood. When people hear the word "leader," they picture someone with a title—class president, team captain, or CEO. Titles make leadership seem official, like something you must earn before making a difference. But here's the truth: leadership has nothing to do with titles and everything to do with actions.

The people with the most significant impact aren't always the ones with the most authority. They're the ones who step up, often when no one expects them to. Leadership is about influence, not position. It's about the choices you make every day—the way you treat others, the way you approach challenges, and the way you show up when it matters most.

The Unlikely Leader

Let me tell you about Sam. Sam wasn't a captain, a president, or even an officer in any school club. He didn't crave the spotlight. But when disaster struck his community, Sam's quiet leadership became unforgettable.

It was during a spring storm. A massive flood swept through his small town, forcing families to evacuate. The school gym became an emergency shelter filled with families who had lost everything. Sam's family was safe, but something inside him clicked when he saw his neighbors huddled in blankets, unsure what to do next.

Sam gathered his friends without waiting for instructions and started organizing supplies—blankets, water bottles, and snacks. He made lists of what people needed most and walked from group to group, checking on families and offering reassurance.

No one asked him to lead. He didn't have a title or a badge. But when his town needed calm and coordination, Sam stepped up. By the night's end, other volunteers sought guidance from him. The mayor even thanked him personally.

Sam didn't need a title to be a leader. He just needed to act.

Why Actions Speak Louder than Titles

Titles can be impressive but don't automatically make someone a great leader. You've probably seen it yourself—the person with the title who talks a lot but doesn't do much versus the quiet person who leads by example and earns respect.

Authentic leadership comes from your actions and how you make people feel. When you show up, when you follow through, and when you treat others with respect and kindness, people notice. They may not always say it out loud, but they notice.

Think about your school or your team. Who do you look up to? Is it always the person with the loudest voice, or is it the person who listens, takes initiative, and inspires others through their actions?

Why Leading Without a Title is Powerful

When you lead without a title, you lead because you care—not because you're expected to. This makes your leadership more authentic and meaningful. People trust leaders who are motivated by purpose, not ego.

Leading without a title teaches you something important: leadership is earned, not given. You don't need to be the best at everything. You don't need to have all the answers. You need a willingness to step up, try, and learn.

Real-Life Example: The Reluctant Leader

In 2018, a group of middle school students in Chicago noticed that their school didn't have enough after-school programs for creative activities like art and music. Instead of waiting for the school board to fix the issue, they formed a group called "Change Makers" and created their after-school clubs.

The student who led the group wasn't a class president or an honor student—he was a quiet kid named Miles who rarely spoke in class. But everyone turned to Miles when his friends asked who should organize their first meeting. They trusted him because he cared. Miles didn't need a title to make his peers believe in his vision.

By the end of the year, their after-school program had grown to include over 100 students, and the school board officially funded it as a permanent initiative. Miles didn't start out wanting to be a leader, but he became one because he was willing to act.

The Difference Between Power and Influence

Here's a key distinction:

- ❖ *Power: Power comes from a title or authority. Someone might follow orders from a person in power out of obligation.*
- ❖ *Influence: Influence comes from respect and trust. Someone follows an influential leader because they believe in them, not because they have to.*

Titles may give you power, but influence makes you a leader. The best leaders don't rely on their titles—they build influence by being consistent, compassionate, and reliable.

Your Leadership Story Starts Now

How do you lead without a title? You lead by:

* *Helping someone without being asked*
* *Listening when someone needs to be heard*
* *Showing up, even when it's inconvenient*
* *Taking responsibility, even when it's hard*

You may not realize it yet, but people notice the small things you do. Leadership isn't always about grand gestures—it's about the quiet actions that build trust and inspire others.

A Question for You

Think of someone in your life who has influenced you without having an official title. What did they do that made an impact?

Now, ask yourself: *How can I be that person for someone else?*

Your leadership journey has already begun. And remember, you don't need a title to make a difference—you just need the courage to care and the willingness to act.

Building a Foundation of Self-Awareness

Every great leader, whether guiding a sports team, leading a global movement, or mentoring a group of friends, starts with one key trait: self-awareness. You can't lead others until you understand your strengths, weaknesses, motivations, and triggers.

Self-awareness is like having a compass on your leadership journey. Without it, you may find yourself lost and unsure of how to handle conflicts, doubts, or unexpected challenges. But with it, you can navigate the most complicated moments with clarity and confidence.

The Story of Marcus: Knowing What You Bring to the Table

Marcus wasn't the fastest player on the soccer team, and he knew it. But he also knew that he had something else—a strategic mind. While his teammates focused on scoring goals, Marcus could read the field like a chessboard. He knew where the defense was weak when the opposing team would shift positions and how to make a pass at just the right moment.

At first, Marcus felt insecure about not being the fastest or the strongest. But instead of focusing on what he wasn't, he leaned into what he *was*. He became the team's unofficial strategist, helping the coach plan plays and motivating his teammates to think smarter, not just harder. By the end of the season, Marcus wasn't just respected—he was trusted. His self-awareness made him a leader, even though he wasn't the team captain.

The lesson? Leaders don't need to be the best at everything. They need to understand their strengths and use them well.

Why Self-Awareness Matters

When you're self-aware, you:

1. **Recognize your strengths** and know how to use them.
2. **Understand your weaknesses** and ask for help when you need it.
3. **Know your triggers** and learn to stay calm in difficult situations.

Self-awareness helps you avoid one of the biggest traps of leadership: pretending to be something you're not. When you're honest with yourself, you don't waste energy trying to impress others or hide your flaws. Instead, you focus on growth and authenticity.

Blind Spots: What You Don't See Can Hurt You

One of the hardest things about self-awareness is confronting your blind spots—the parts of your personality or habits you're unaware of but that others see clearly. Maybe you interrupt people without realizing it. Perhaps you avoid tough conversations because you're afraid of conflict. Maybe you overcommit because you don't want to let anyone down.

Blind spots don't make you a lousy leader—they make you human. The key is being open to feedback. Leaders who are willing to listen and learn from others to become stronger.

The Power of Honest Reflection

Take a moment to reflect on yourself as a leader:

❖ *When do you feel most confident?*
❖ *What kinds of situations make you nervous or unsure?*

❖ *How do you handle criticism or failure?*

Self-reflection isn't always comfortable, but it's one of the fastest-growing methods. Leaders who reflect on their actions are better prepared for the next challenge because they've learned from their experiences.

How to Build Self-Awareness

Here are a few ways you can strengthen your self-awareness:

1. **Keep a Leadership Journal**: At the end of each day or week, write down moments where you led, made a mistake, or handled a challenging situation. Reflect on what went well and what you could improve.

2. **Ask for Feedback**: Choose people you trust—friends, teachers, coaches—and ask them for honest feedback. You might learn something surprising about how you come across to others.

3. **Pay Attention to Your Emotions**: When you feel frustrated, anxious, or excited, take a moment to ask yourself: *Why do I feel this way?* Understanding your emotions helps you control your reactions.

4. **Celebrate Your Wins**: Self-awareness isn't just about fixing weaknesses—it's also about recognizing your strengths. When you handle something well, give yourself credit.

The Self-Aware Leader

Self-awareness doesn't mean you have to have everything figured out. It means you're honest with yourself and willing to grow. Leaders who know themselves don't pretend to be invincible—they're real, and that authenticity makes people trust them.

By building a foundation of self-awareness, you're setting yourself up for success—not just in leadership, but in life. When you understand who you are and what you bring to the table, you confidently step into every situation, no matter how challenging.

Your Challenge

This week, I take five minutes each day to reflect on one leadership moment—big or small. Write down what you did well and what you could improve. Over time, you'll start to see patterns—your strengths, your blind spots, and your areas for growth.

Remember: leadership starts with knowing yourself. And when you know yourself, you can lead others with empathy, confidence, and purpose.

Leadership as Influence and Responsibility

Leadership isn't about giving orders—it's about earning trust. It's about how you make people feel, the example you set, and the sense of purpose you create. At its core, leadership is influence. But with influence comes responsibility—the responsibility to lead with integrity, fairness, and respect.

When people think of influence, they often picture someone with charisma—someone who can captivate a room with their words. But real influence doesn't rely on charm alone. Actual influence is built over time through consistent actions and a reputation for doing what's right, even when it's hard.

The Story of Mia: Earning Trust One Step at a Time

Mia was voted captain of her school's volleyball team during her junior year. On paper, she had everything—talent, confidence, and an intense game record. But something was missing: trust. Some of her teammate's felt Mia was only focused on herself—her stats, wins, and performance.

Mia didn't realize how much her leadership role required her to show up for her team, not just on the court but in small, everyday moments. Mia initially felt defensive when her coach sat her down and shared this feedback. But then she thought about what kind of leader she wanted to be. She realized that the captain wasn't just about scoring points and lifting others.

Mia arrived early to practice the next day and stayed late to help her teammates with drills. She started asking how they felt after games, celebrating their wins—even the small ones. Slowly but surely, the energy on the team shifted. By the end of the season, her team wasn't just more substantial—they trusted each other. Mia learned that leadership isn't about being the best player; it's about making everyone feel seen and supported.

The Ripple Effect of Influence

Every time you make a choice, you're influencing someone—whether you realize it or not. The way you treat people, the way you handle stress, the way you show up when things get tough—all of these actions create a ripple effect.

Think about the last time someone showed you kindness when you didn't expect it. How did that moment impact your day?

Maybe it inspired you to pass that kindness along to someone else. That's influence in action.

Now think about the opposite—times when someone acted unfairly or dismissively. How did that feel? Those moments remind us that influence can be positive or negative. As a leader, you ensure your influence lifts others rather than bringing them down.

What Responsibility Means

Being responsible as a leader doesn't mean you have to be perfect. It means being accountable—not just for your successes but also for your mistakes. It means owning your actions, learning from your failures, and striving to improve.

Imagine you're leading a group project. If something goes wrong—maybe a deadline is missed, or the presentation isn't polished—it's easy to point fingers. But real leaders resist that temptation. Instead, they ask, *what could I have done differently? How can we fix this together?*

Responsibility also means being aware of how your words and decisions affect others. It means asking yourself, *Am I making this decision for the right reasons? Am I considering how this will impact everyone involved?*

The Temptation of Power

One of the most complex parts of leadership is resisting the urge to use your influence for the wrong reasons. When people look up to you, it can be tempting to prioritize your own goals over what's best for the group.

History is filled with leaders who started with good intentions but lost their way because they let power cloud their judgment. That's why staying grounded in your values is so important. Leaders who lead with integrity understand that influence isn't about control but service.

The Balance between Confidence and Humility

Great leaders strike a balance between confidence and humility. They're confident enough to take charge when needed but humble enough to admit when they're wrong and listen to others.

Humility doesn't mean thinking less of yourself—it means recognizing that you don't have all the answers and being open to learning. Confident leaders with humility make people feel safe, respected, and inspired.

Influence in Everyday Moments

You don't need to be a captain, president, or manager to have influence. Influence happens in everyday moments:

❖ *When you include someone who feels left out.*
❖ *When you admit a mistake instead of covering it up.*
❖ *When you step up and take responsibility for something no one else wants to handle.*

The more you practice these moments of influence, the stronger your leadership becomes.

Your Leadership Challenge

Think about a situation where you've had the chance to influence someone's experience. Maybe you helped a struggling friend or took the lead in a group assignment. Now, think about how you can grow that influence by focusing on your actions and how they affect others.

Remember: leadership is a privilege, not a right. It's about using your influence to improve things for the people around you. When you lead with responsibility, you don't just earn respect—you build trust, and that trust becomes the foundation of lasting influence.

Reflection – What Kind of Leader Do You Want to Be?

Close your eyes and picture the kind of leader you admire. Is it someone who stands before a crowd and inspires people with their words? Or someone who quietly leads by example, making everyone feel included and valued? Maybe it's someone who stood by you when you felt alone—someone who made you believe in yourself.

Now, take a moment and imagine yourself in that role. What does your leadership look like? How do you make people feel? What do you stand for?

One of the most powerful questions you can ask yourself is this: *What kind of leader do I want to be?*

This isn't about imitating someone else or checking off boxes—it's about figuring out what drives you, what you believe in, and how you want to show up in the world.

The Leaders We Remember

Think about the leaders whose stories stay with you—the ones whose names echo through history books, documentaries, and conversations. What makes them unforgettable isn't just what they accomplished—it's how they led and who they were at their core.

Martin Luther King Jr.'s leadership wasn't just about powerful speeches but his unshakable commitment to justice and nonviolence. Malala Yousafzai's leadership wasn't about fame but her courage to stand up for girls' education, even when her life was on the line.

These leaders didn't follow a script or a formula. They knew who they were, what they valued, and what they wanted to change. Their leadership was an extension of their values.

You don't have to be on a global stage to lead purposefully. Leadership starts with understanding what matters most to you and finding ways to live those values daily.

The Power of Self-Definition

When you don't define yourself as a leader, the world will try to define it for you. People might assume you should lead a certain way because of your personality—whether you're shy, bold, quiet, or outspoken. But leadership doesn't fit into neat categories.

Some leaders inspire through their words; others lead by listening. Some leaders are detail-focused problem-solvers; others are big-picture visionaries. The key is to figure out what works for *you*. There's no one-size-fits-all mold.

So, take ownership of your leadership identity. Ask yourself:

❖ *Do I lead by speaking up or by creating space for others to speak?*
❖ *Do I shine in one-on-one conversations or group settings?*

❖ *Do I enjoy solving logistical challenges, or am I drawn to creative brainstorming?*

Once you understand your natural style, you can build on it and grow into the leader you're meant to be.

Your Values Are Your Compass

Every great leader is guided by their values—principles that help them make tough decisions, stay grounded during setbacks, and remain consistent in their actions. When you lead without clear values, it's easy to lose your way.

Think of your values as a compass that points you toward your true north. When faced with a difficult choice—standing up for someone being mistreated or speaking out in a group when it feels risky—your values remind you of who you are and what you stand for.

To discover your values, start by asking yourself:

❖ *What matters most to me?*
❖ *What do I want people to remember about me as a leader?*
❖ *What behaviors make me feel proud of myself?*

You might value honesty, empathy, resilience, creativity, or fairness. Your values are unique to you and shape the kind of leader you'll become.

The Leader You're Becoming

You won't have all the answers right away—and that's okay. Leadership isn't about perfection; it's about progress. The more you reflect on your leadership style and values, the more intentional you'll become.

Think of your leadership journey like building a playlist. Each song you add represents a part of your identity—the lessons you've learned, the people who've inspired you, and the goals you've set for yourself. Over time, your leadership "playlist" grows into something meaningful and personal—a reflection of who you are.

Reflection Exercise: Create Your Leadership Profile

Take some time to reflect and write out your answers to the following prompts:

1. **Leadership Role Model**: Who's a leader you admire, and why?
2. **Your Strengths**: What are three things you're naturally good at?
3. **Your Values**: What three values guide the way you want to lead?
4. **Your Goals**: What's one leadership goal you want to achieve this year?

When you're done, look over your answers. You've just created your first leadership profile—a snapshot of the kind of leader you're becoming.

A Note for Your Future Self

Imagine yourself five years from now. What will you remember about your leadership journey? You probably won't remember every detail of the projects you led or the speeches you gave. You'll remember when you stayed true to yourself—when you spoke up for what was right, supported someone who needed it, or learned from your mistakes.

Leadership isn't about becoming someone new—it's about becoming more of who you already are. The best leaders know themselves, believe in themselves and lead with purpose.

So, take a deep breath and ask yourself: *What kind of leader do I want to be?* Then, step forward and start becoming that person today.

CHAPTER 2

THE FEAR OF SPEAKING AND HOW TO OVERCOME IT

It's the moment you've been dreading. Your name is called. You stand up, your heart pounding like a drum, your palms clammy, and your throat dry. You walk to the front of the room, but instead of thinking about what you want to say, all you can focus on is one thought: *What if I mess up?*

If you've ever felt this way, you're not alone. Fear of public speaking is one of the most common fears in the world—even more than the fear of heights or spiders. Studies show that up to 77% of people experience anxiety about speaking in front of others. But here's the secret, great speakers know fear isn't something you have to eliminate—it's something you can learn to work with.

The First Speech: Sarah's Story

Sarah had always been terrified of public speaking. Sarah felt sick when her history teacher announced that everyone must present a five-minute speech. She couldn't picture anything more nerve-wracking than standing in front of her classmates, all eyes on her, waiting for her to make a mistake.

But something changed when she finally gave her speech. She stumbled over her words at first, her hands shaking as she held her notecards. But halfway through, she noticed something surprising, people were listening. A few classmates nodded in agreement as she spoke. She paused, breathed, and finished her speech more confidently.

Her heart was still racing when she sat back down, but she felt something new: pride. She had faced her fear and survived. More than that—she had *grown*.

Why Do We Fear Public Speaking?

The fear of speaking in front of others often comes down to one thing: the fear of judgment. What if I forget my words? What if people laugh? What if I look foolish? These "what ifs" play on a loop until we convince ourselves that speaking in public is a guaranteed disaster.

But here's the truth: most audience members aren't waiting for you to fail. They want you to succeed. Think about the last time you watched someone give a speech. Were you picking apart their every mistake or hoping they'd inspire you? Often, audiences root for the speaker, not against them.

Turning Fear into Fuel

Fear doesn't have to stop you—it can make you a better speaker. When your heart is racing, it's your body's way of giving you energy. Public speaking is like stepping onto a stage before a race. Your nerves are proof that you care. When you learn to channel that energy, you can turn fear into focus.

Practical Steps to Overcome Fear

1. **Breathe Deeply**: When you're nervous, your breaths become shallow, which makes you feel even more anxious. Practice taking slow, deep breaths before you speak—inhale for four seconds, hold for four seconds, and exhale for four seconds. This calms your body and clears your mind.

2. **Prepare, but Don't Over-Rehearse**: The more familiar you are with your speech, the more confident you'll feel. But don't try to memorize every word. Focus on key points so that if you forget something, you can keep going naturally.

3. **Picture a Friendly Face**: When speaking, find someone in the audience who looks supportive—a friend, a teacher, or even someone nodding along. Imagine you're talking directly to them. This makes the experience feel more like a conversation than a performance.

4. **Embrace the Pause**: One of the scariest things about public speaking is silence. But pauses can make your speech more powerful. When you pause after an important point, you give your audience time to absorb your message and give yourself a chance to breathe and reset.

The Power of Progress

You won't give a flawless speech on your first try—and that's okay. Great speakers aren't born—they're made through practice, patience, and persistence. Every time you speak, you build a skill set that will serve you for the rest of your life.

Think of public speaking as a muscle. The more you exercise it, the stronger it becomes. Your first speech might feel shaky, but your tenth speech will feel stronger, and your fiftieth speech? You might even look forward to it.

The Most Important Lesson

Remember: public speaking isn't about being perfect—it's about being *authentic*. Robots don't deliver the best speeches; they're offered by people who connect with their audience. It's okay to pause, to breathe, to stumble and recover. Your audience will remember your sincerity, not your mistakes.

Your Challenge

This week, find a small moment to practice speaking— whether volunteering to answer a question in class, speaking up in a group project, or sharing an idea at home. Start with something small and build from there. Each time you speak, remind yourself: *I don't have to be perfect. I just have to be authentic.*

The more you practice, the quieter your fears will become. One day, you'll realize that the voice telling you, "*You can't do this*" has been replaced by a new voice—a stronger, more confident one that says, "I've *got this.*"

Structuring an Engaging Speech

Imagine this: You're in the audience at a school assembly. The speaker on stage starts reading from their paper in a monotone voice. You glance at the clock and wonder how long you'll have to sit through it. You zone out after a few minutes and start thinking about lunch instead.

Now, picture a different scene. The next speaker steps onto the stage, takes a deep breath, and says, *"Do you remember the first time you failed at something?"* Suddenly, you're paying attention. You're thinking about your own life, not just listening to words. The speaker pulls you into a story that makes you nod along, smile, or even hold your breath. When they finish, you don't just remember their words—you remember how they made you feel.

The difference between those two speakers wasn't just confidence but structure. A great speech isn't just a collection of facts or ideas. It's a journey with a beginning, middle, and end.

The Secret Sauce of Great Speeches

Consider some of the most famous speeches in history—Martin Luther King Jr.'s "I Have a Dream," Malala Yousafzai's address at the United Nations, and Steve Jobs' commencement speech at Stanford. What made those speeches unforgettable wasn't just what they said but *how* they said it. They took the audience on a ride filled with anticipation, emotion, and resolution.

So, how can you build a speech that sticks with your audience? Let's break it down.

Step 1: The Hook (Grab Their Attention)

Your first few sentences are like the opening scene of a movie—they set the tone and determine whether your audience will stick with you or tune out. A strong hook makes people sit up and think, *"Wait, this is different. I need to pay attention."*

There are several ways to start a speech:

- ❖ **Ask**: *"What's the one thing you'd change about your school if you could?"*
- ❖ **Tell a Story**: *"I thought I could fly when I thought I could fly. Here's how that turned out."*
- ❖ **Share a Surprising Fact**: *"Did you know that the average person spends 90,000 hours at work in their lifetime? That's a third of their life."*

The goal is to pull your audience in from the first sentence and make them curious.

Step 2: The Core Message (What Do You Want Them to Remember?)

Every great speech has one central idea—the message that stays with people long after they've left the room. This isn't a place to list every fact or idea you've ever had. Instead, ask yourself: *If my audience only remembers one thing, what should it be?*

In Steve Jobs' famous commencement speech, his core message was clear: *Follow your passion and trust that the dots will connect.* He reinforced that message with personal stories about failure, resilience, and finding purpose.

When you build your core message, keep it simple. One idea, one focus. Everything else in your speech should support that message.

Step 3: The Heartbeat (Why Should They Care?)

Logic can convince people, but emotion moves them. Once you've shared your core message, it's time to make them feel something. This is where personal stories, vivid imagery, and real-life examples come into play.

Take Malala's UN speech, for example. She didn't just list statistics about education inequality. She shared her story of surviving a tragedy and standing up for what she believed in. That made her words unforgettable—it wasn't just information, it was inspiration.

To find your speech's heartbeat, ask yourself:

❖ *What personal experience connects to this message?*
❖ *How can I show my audience the impact of this issue instead of just telling them about it?*

Step 4: The Call to Action (What Should They Do?)

A speech without a call to action is like a movie without an ending. You've captured your audience's attention, shared your message, and made them care—now what? What's the next step?

Your call to action doesn't have to be dramatic. It could be as simple as:

❖ *"Talk to someone today who you've never spoken to before."*
❖ *"Sign up to volunteer at the community drive next weekend."*
❖ *"Think about what courage means to you and write it down."*

The point is to leave your audience with something to do, remember, or reflect on.

The Story of Lily: How Structure Saved Her Speech

Lily had always been full of ideas, but her speeches? A mess. She'd start with one thought, jump to another, forget a key point, and then rushed to the end. She knew she was losing her audience halfway through but didn't know how to fix it.

Her speech teacher challenged her to **write her core message in one sentence and build everything around it.** Lily's message was simple: *Small acts of kindness can change someone's life.* With that focus, she reworked her speech.

She opened with a story about a stranger who helped her when she got lost in a new city. She shared facts about kindness, but only to support her story. And at the end, she challenged her classmates: "Be that person for someone else today."

The room was quiet when Lily finished—not because they were bored, but because they were thinking. Her speech didn't just inform them—it inspired them.

Why Structure Sets You Free

Some people think structure makes speeches sound robotic or forced. But in reality, the structure gives you freedom. Knowing your beginning, middle, and end makes you less likely to get lost or overwhelmed. Instead of worrying about what comes next, you can focus on connecting with your audience.

Your Speech Blueprint

Before your next presentation, ask yourself:

1. **Hook**: How will I grab their attention?
2. **Core Message**: What's the one thing I want them to remember?
3. **Heartbeat**: How can I make them care?
4. **Call to Action**: What should they do after hearing my speech?

Write it down, practice it, and remind yourself: *This is my story, and I'm ready to share it.*

The Power of Storytelling

People may forget your words but they will never forget how you make them feel. And nothing makes people feel more than a great story.

Think about the best speeches you've ever heard. What made them stick? Was it the facts and statistics or the story behind them? Stories are how we make sense of the world. They're how we connect, remember, and believe. If you can tell a story well, you can capture hearts, change minds, and leave a lasting impact.

The "Campfire Effect"

For thousands of years, humans have gathered around fires to tell stories—about survival, dreams, and heroes. Why? Because stories have the power to transport us. When someone tells a good story, we aren't just listening—imagining, feeling, and experiencing.

Your speech, ideas, and message need a story at their center. A story creates something called the "campfire effect." It pulls people in, makes them lean closer, and makes them *feel* something. It doesn't matter whether you're in front of 10 friends in a classroom or a crowd of hundreds. A well-told story turns your audience into a circle of listeners around a fire.

The Anatomy of a Great Story

Every great story has three essential parts:

1. **The Hook (Set the Scene)**: A great story begins with a moment that makes your audience lean in.
   a. *"The summer I turned 13, I broke my arm doing something incredibly stupid."*
   b. *"When I was 10, I made a mistake that cost my soccer team the championship."*
2. **The Struggle (The Challenge)**: This is the heart of your story—the obstacle, the conflict, or the challenge you faced.
   a. *"We were losing by two points with 30 seconds left on the clock."*
   b. *"My best friend stopped talking to me, and I had no idea why."*
3. **The Resolution (What You Learned or Achieved)**: End with the moment where everything changed—the lesson, the victory, or the realization.
   a. *"In that moment, I realized that failing doesn't make you weak—it makes you human."*

b. *"I finally found the courage to apologize, which saved our friendship."*

The Story of Caleb: Winning the Crowd

Caleb wasn't the most vigorous debater on his team. His arguments were solid, but he struggled to connect with the audience. During one competition, he noticed that his opponents weren't just presenting facts but telling stories. They weren't saying, "Climate change is an issue because temperatures are rising." They said, "Meet Maria, a mother in a coastal town whose home was destroyed by rising sea levels."

It clicked for Caleb. At his next debate, he told a personal story about volunteering at a local shelter after a storm. He described what it felt like to see families who had lost everything. The judges weren't just nodding along—they were emotionally invested. Caleb didn't just present an argument—he painted a picture. And he won.

Why Stories Work

Stories make facts stick. Psychologists call this the "narrative transportation effect." When you tell a story, you activate the parts of the brain that process memories, emotions, and even senses like sight and sound. Suddenly, your audience isn't just listening—they're *feeling* your story as if it's happening to them.

Think of it this way: if you give someone a list of reasons why they should care about an issue, they might remember a few facts. But if you tell them a story that makes them laugh, cry, or gasp? They'll remember the story—and everything it taught them.

How to Find Your Story

You don't need a dramatic life event to tell a great story. Some of the best stories come from small, everyday moments:

- ❖ *The time you helped a friend who was having a rough day.*
- ❖ *The time you stood up for something you believed in, even when it felt uncomfortable.*
- ❖ *A challenge you faced—big or small—and how you grew because of it.*
- ❖ *Ask yourself:*
- ❖ *What's a moment that changed the way I see the world?*
- ❖ *What's an experience that taught me something I'll never forget?*
- ❖ *What's a time when I failed but came out stronger?*

Your story doesn't have to be perfect—it must be accurate.

Bringing Your Audience into the Story

Once you've chosen your story, bring your audience into it. Make them see what you saw, feel what you felt. Instead of saying, "I was nervous," say:

- ❖ *"My hands were shaking, my heart was pounding, and my stomach felt like it was doing somersaults."*
- ❖ *Instead of saying, "I was happy," describe the moment:*

❖ *"The second the buzzer sounded, my teammates swarmed me, and I couldn't stop smiling. It felt like the world had slowed down for just a second."*

The more specific and sensory your descriptions, the more your audience will connect with your story.

The Hero of Your Story

Here's an important tip: you don't have to be the hero in your story. Sometimes, the most powerful stories are about someone who inspired you—a coach, a friend, a sibling, or even a stranger. What matters is the emotion behind the story and the lesson you're sharing.

Your Storytelling Challenge

This week, write down one meaningful story from your life that taught you a lesson or changed your perspective. Practice telling it to someone you trust. Pay attention to their reaction—when do they lean in? When do they smile or ask questions?

Your story doesn't have to be perfect, and neither do you. The best stories are the ones that come from the heart, not from a script.

The power of storytelling isn't just about what you say—it's about how you make people feel. And when you make people feel something, you create a connection that lasts long after the words have ended.

Handling Q&A and Unexpected Situations

Imagine this: You've just finished giving your speech. The applause hasn't even died when someone raises their hand with a question that feels like a curveball aimed straight at your confidence. Your heart skips a beat. *What if I don't know the answer? What if they're trying to trip me up?*

No matter how prepared or experienced, every speaker faces moments like this. Handling questions and unexpected situations is one of the most intimidating parts of public speaking—but it's also one of the most powerful. When you can navigate these moments gracefully and confidently, you show your audience that you're knowledgeable and resilient.

The Spotlight Moment: Alex's Challenge

Alex was in the middle of presenting his research project on ocean conservation. He had rehearsed every slide and practiced his speech so many times he could practically recite it in his sleep. But during the Q&A, a classmate raised a hand and asked a question Alex hadn't prepared for:

"Why should we care about ocean conservation when there are so many other urgent problems worldwide?"

Alex felt his mind go blank. For a split second, doubt crept in. He could feel the room holding its breath. But instead of panicking, Alex took a deep breath, smiled, and said, *"That's a great question. And it's true—there are a lot of important problems in the world. But think about this: the oceans cover more than 70% of our planet. When they suffer, it affects everything—from food to weather patterns to wildlife. So, by protecting the oceans, we protect more than just water."*

His response wasn't rehearsed—it was real. And that made it even more powerful. The applause that followed wasn't just for his research but for his calm, thoughtful response in a high-pressure moment.

Why Q&A Can Feel Scary (and How to Reframe It)

Your brain loves patterns. When you practice your speech, your brain gets used to the flow—the intro, the main points, the conclusion. But when someone throws a question, your brain feels like the pattern has been disrupted. Suddenly, it's unpredictable.

But here's the thing: questions aren't interruptions—they're *opportunities*. When someone asks you a question, they allow you to show that you know your stuff and can think on your feet. Instead of viewing questions as obstacles, start viewing them as proof that people are engaged and curious.

The Power of Pausing

One of the biggest mistakes people make when answering questions is feeling the need to respond immediately. But here's a secret: silence isn't your enemy—it's your tool.

When asked a tricky question, pause for a few seconds before answering. This pause serves two purposes:

1. It gives your brain time to process and form a clear answer.
2. It signals to your audience that you're thoughtful and composed.

Pausing doesn't make you look unprepared—it makes you look intentional.

Types of Questions and How to Handle Them

1. **The Curious Question**: These questions come from genuine curiosity. The person asking wants to know more.
    a. *Example*: "Can you explain how your idea would work in real life?"
    b. **How to Respond**: Smile and treat the question as a compliment—it means your audience is engaged—answer in a way that adds value without overwhelming them with too much information.
2. **The Challenging Question**: Sometimes, people ask questions that feel like criticism or pushback.
    a. *Example*: "Don't you think your solution is too expensive?"
    b. **How to Respond**: Stay calm and avoid being defensive. Acknowledge their point but steer the conversation back to your message.
    c. *Response*: "That's a fair point. Cost is a challenge, but one way to make it more affordable is by starting small and scaling up."
3. **The Off-Topic Question**: Some questions can feel completely unrelated.

a. *Example*: "What's your favorite movie?" (in the middle of a speech about leadership)

b. **How to Respond**: Bring the Focus back without dismissing the person.

c. *Response*: "Great question! And while I could talk about movies all day, let's circle back to leadership—because that's the real story here."

4. **The "I Don't Know" Question**: The most challenging question is the one you don't know the answer to.

a. **How to Respond**: Admitting when you don't know something is okay. No one expects you to have all the answers. The key is how you handle it.

b. *Response*: "That's an important question, and I don't have the exact answer right now. But I'd love to research it and get back to you."

Staying Composed When Things Go Off Script

It's not just questions that can throw you off—unexpected moments. The projector doesn't work. Someone interrupts you. You forget your place.

The best way to stay calm in these situations is to focus on what you *can* control:

❖ *Your Breathing: Slow, deep breaths keep you grounded.*

❖ *Your Perspective: Mistakes feel more significant to you than they do to your audience. Most people won't even notice if you keep moving forward.*

❖ **Your Attitude**: *Treat unexpected moments as part of the story. If the microphone cuts out, joke about it. If you lose your place, pause, smile, and say, "Let me back up for a second."*

Audiences admire speakers who can handle chaos with grace. It makes you relatable—and even more memorable.

The Confidence Equation

Confidence in Q&A sessions comes from two things:

1. **Preparation**: The more familiar you are with your topic, the more confident you'll feel.
2. **Presence**: Staying present in the moment helps you stay calm and adaptable, no matter what comes your way.

Remember, your goal isn't to have all the answers—it's to create a conversation. When you show your audience that you're open, calm, and curious, they'll see you as someone worth listening to—not just because of what you say, but because of how you say it.

Your Challenge

The next time you're in class, try raising your hand to answer a question, even if you're not 100% sure of your answer. Practice speaking up in small, low-pressure moments to build your comfort level.

Then, practice answering questions out loud—even if it's just with a family member or a friend. Have them ask you tough, random questions to simulate what it feels like to think on your feet.

Your goal isn't to have perfect answers—it's to get comfortable being *in the moment*. Because the best speakers aren't the ones who never mess up—they're the ones who know how to bounce back.

Practice Makes Perfect – Building Confidence Over Time

Public speaking isn't a talent that some people are born with—it's a skill. And like any skill, it gets better with practice. Think about learning to ride a bike. The first time, you wobbled, maybe fell and wondered if you'd ever figure it out. But after practicing repeatedly, you gained balance and confidence, and eventually, you didn't even have to think about it—you just rode.

Public speaking is the same. The more you practice, the more natural it feels. What once felt terrifying can eventually become exciting—or even fun.

The Myth of "Perfect" Speakers

Many think the best speakers just step on stage and deliver flawless speeches without sweat. But behind every confident speech you've heard are hours of preparation, mistakes, and practice. Even the most famous public speakers have had moments where they froze, forgot their lines, or faced rejection.

The difference is that they didn't stop. They learned, adjusted, and tried again.

One of the most powerful lessons in public speaking is that your first attempt doesn't define you. Whether you crush it or crash, it's part of the process.

The Story of Jordan: From Fear to Flow

Jordan was asked to deliver a speech at her school's leadership assembly. It wasn't a huge audience—just a couple of hundred classmates and teachers—but it felt like a stadium to her. The first time she rehearsed her speech in front of her family, she stumbled over her words, forgot a section entirely, and blurted out, "This is the worst idea ever!" before running out of the room.

But Jordan's mom followed her, handed her a water bottle, and said, *"Do it again."* Jordan wanted to say no. She was embarrassed, and the last thing she wanted was to repeat what felt like a disaster. But something in her mom's calm voice made her take a breath and nod. She went back in, tried again, and improved just a little.

By the fifth time, she wasn't shaking anymore. By the tenth, she felt proud of how far she'd come. When she finally stood on that stage, she didn't just recite her speech—she owned it.

The assembly wasn't just a presentation for Jordan—it was proof that practice turns fear into flow.

The Science of Confidence

Confidence isn't magic—it's muscle memory. When you practice something enough times, your brain builds new connections that make it easier to perform that task. Neuroscientists call this "myelin insulation"—every time you repeat an action; your brain creates stronger and faster pathways to accomplish it.

Think of your first few speeches as building reps at the gym. The first rep feels awkward and heavy, but each time you lift, you're building strength.

Why Repetition Matters

Practice isn't just about repeating your speech but refining it. Here's how practice makes your speech stronger over time:

1. **Clarity**: The more you practice, the more precise your message becomes. You start to trim unnecessary words and focus on your key points.
2. **Flow**: Practice helps you find the natural rhythm of your speech—the pauses, the emphasis, the build-up to your main ideas.
3. **Recovery**: By practicing, you prepare yourself for real-life scenarios. If you mess up during practice, you learn how to recover, so when it happens live, you won't panic.

Making Practice Count

Not all practice is equal. To build absolute confidence, your practice sessions should push you just a little outside your comfort zone. Here's how to make your practice sessions more effective:

1. **Practice Out Loud**: Reading your speech silently in your head isn't the same as speaking it aloud. Your brain

processes language differently when you hear yourself say, so practice as if you're performing.

2. **Record Yourself**: It can feel awkward initially, but recording yourself helps you catch things you might not notice—like speaking too fast or using filler words like "um" or "like."

3. **Change the Setting**: Don't always practice in the same room. Try practicing outside, in your classroom, or in front of a mirror. Changing your environment helps you adapt to new surroundings.

4. **Simulate Stress**: Practice with friends or family who can give you feedback. If you get nervous, that's okay—it's the closest thing to the experience and helps you build resilience.

Learning to Laugh at Mistakes

One of the most essential lessons in public speaking is this: mistakes don't define your speech—you do. You have a choice if you mispronounce a word, forget a line or trip to the podium. You can let the mistake unravel you or laugh it off and keep going.

Audiences love authenticity. If you smile and say, *"Well, that wasn't part of the plan!"* and keep moving, they'll be on your side.

The Power of Visualization

In addition to practice, visualization is a powerful tool. Close your eyes and picture yourself giving your speech. Imagine walking up, seeing your audience, and hearing your strong, clear voice. Picture the audience nodding, clapping, and connecting with your words.

Visualization isn't just daydreaming—it helps your brain rehearse success. The more vividly you imagine yourself succeeding, the more your brain believes you can.

Your Confidence Timeline

Here's something to remember confidence doesn't happen overnight. It's built speech by speech, practice by practice. You might start with small wins—raising your hand in class, leading a group discussion—and work up to more significant moments, like giving a speech at an event or leading a meeting.

By taking small, consistent steps, you're training your brain to feel comfortable with being seen and heard.

Your Practice Challenge

This week, choose one small speaking goal:

❖ *Answering a question in class.*
❖ *Presenting an idea to your family at dinner.*
❖ *Practicing a speech out loud for five minutes.*

After each attempt, reflect on what went well and what you can improve. Remind yourself that progress, not perfection, is the goal.

One day, without realizing it, you'll step in front of an audience and feel something new—not fear, but excitement. And at that moment, you'll know that all the practice was worth it.

Finding Your Voice – Speaking with Authenticity

No matter how polished or rehearsed, every great speech comes down to one essential thing: authenticity. The most influential speakers aren't the ones who sound like they've memorized every word from a textbook. They're the ones who speak with honesty, vulnerability, and confidence in their unique voice.

But what does "finding your voice" really mean? It's not about speaking the loudest or having the perfect vocabulary. It's about embracing yourself—your stories, experiences, and perspectives—and authentically sharing them.

The Story of Aiden: When Imitation Fails

Aiden was determined to win in his first year on the debate team. He watched videos of championship debaters and tried to copy their style—their gestures, tone, and catchphrases. But something felt off when he finally stepped up for his first round. His words came out flat, and he stumbled through his points.

He lost the debate. Worse than that, he felt like a fraud.

Afterward, his coach pulled him aside and said, *"Stop trying to be someone else. Speak the way you speak. Your voice matters, not theirs."*

At the next competition, Aiden ditched the over-the-top gestures and rehearsed catchphrases. He spoke simply but with passion. Instead of trying to impress the judges, he focused on making his message clear and heartfelt. He didn't just win the round—he earned a standing ovation.

Aiden's victory wasn't just about the debate but about realizing that his authentic voice was his greatest strength.

Why Your Voice Matters

In a world filled with social media filters and highlight reels, it can feel like everyone is trying to be a version of someone else. But here's the thing: people crave authenticity. They're drawn to real stories, genuine emotions, and authentic connections.

When you speak with your authentic voice, you give people something rare—a glimpse into who you are. And that's what makes your words memorable.

Avoiding the "Perfection Trap"

One of the biggest obstacles to finding your voice is the pressure to sound "perfect." You might worry about saying the wrong thing, mispronouncing a word, or forgetting a point. But guess what? No one expects you to be perfect.

Perfection isn't relatable authenticity is. Your audience isn't looking for a flawless performance. They're looking for someone who speaks with honesty and heart. If you stumble, smile, and keep going. If you lose your place, take a deep breath, and pick up where you left off.

Authentic speakers don't let mistakes stop them—they turn those moments into proof that they're human.

What Makes Your Voice Unique

Your experiences, beliefs, and personality shape your voice. Ask yourself:

❖ *What do I care about most?*
❖ *What stories from my life have shaped who I am?*
❖ *What values do I stand by?*

The answers to these questions make your voice different from anyone else's. You don't have to sound like a famous speaker or influencer—you just have to sound like *you*.

The "Best Friend" Technique

Here's a trick for speaking authentically: imagine you're talking to your best friend. When you talk to someone you trust, you're more relaxed, honest, and yourself. Try bringing that same energy to your speeches.

When standing in front of an audience, picture a familiar, friendly face in the crowd. Speak to that person the way you'd speak to someone who knows you inside and out. This can make your tone warmer, your delivery more natural, and your confidence stronger.

The Story That Only You Can Tell

Every person has a story that only they can tell. Your experiences—the challenges you've overcome, the lessons you've learned, the dreams you've chased—are uniquely yours. These stories are your superpower as a speaker.

When Priya shared her story about struggling to fit in after moving to a new school, she didn't sugarcoat the experience. She talked about loneliness, the awkward first days, and the moment someone finally invited her to sit at their lunch table. She spoke from the heart, and half the room was tearing up by the time she finished.

No one else could've told that story the way Priya did—because it was hers. And that's what made it powerful.

Breaking Free from Comparison

One of the biggest traps teenagers fall into is comparing themselves to others. *Why don't I sound as confident as him? Why don't I have stories like hers?* But comparison only takes you further away from your authentic voice.

Instead of focusing on what you're not, focus on what you are:

❖ *What makes you curious?*
❖ *What lights you up?*
❖ *What challenges have shaped your perspective?*

Your voice isn't meant to sound like anyone else's. It's meant to be yours.

Your Authenticity Practice

This week, I will practice speaking the truth by telling someone a story that means something to you. It doesn't have to be long or dramatic—just honest. Share something that made you laugh, cry, or think differently.

Pay attention to how they react. Did they lean in? Did they smile? Chances are, they connected with you because you spoke from the heart, not a script.

Your Voice is Enough

The world doesn't need more perfect speakers—it needs more authentic ones. When you speak with your true voice, you don't just deliver information—you build connection, trust, and impact.

The next time you speak, remind yourself: *My voice matters. My story matters. And I don't need to sound like anyone else—I just need to be real.*

CHAPTER 3

THE BASICS OF DEBATE

Imagine standing in front of an audience, your heart racing but your mind razor-sharp. Across from you is your opponent, ready to challenge everything you say. It's not a fight—it's a conversation built on logic, creativity, and passion. This is the world of debate—where words become your most potent tools and ideas clash, not to tear each other down but to reveal the truth.

But if you've never debated, it can feel like stepping into a foreign world. What are the rules? How do you know when to speak? How do you win? Don't worry—we're about to break it all down in a way that makes sense.

Why Debate Matters

Before we dive into formats and rules, let's talk about why debate is such an important skill. Debate isn't just about winning arguments—it's about learning to think critically, communicate clearly, and listen actively.

Here's what makes debate different from a regular argument:

❖ *In a discussion, you're not just speaking—you're listening. You're looking for holes in your opponent's argument, not to "destroy" them, but to strengthen your reasoning.*

❖ *A debate teaches you to see both sides of an issue. You may be assigned to argue about a side you don't personally agree with, and that's part of the challenge. It forces you to understand perspectives different from your own—and that's a powerful skill in life.*

The Story of Ella: A Lesson in Perspective

Ella was a passionate environmentalist who loved speaking up about the dangers of climate change. When she joined her school's debate team, she expected to win every round when assigned her usual position: arguing for stronger environmental laws. But then, one day, her coach threw her a curveball—Ella was asked to argue *against* government restrictions on emissions.

At first, she was furious. How could she argue about something she disagreed with? However, as she researched, she learned more about how industries could be incentivized to change voluntarily and how specific regulations, if poorly designed, could hurt small businesses.

When Ella finally stood before the judges, she argued her side with clarity and respect. She didn't change her personal beliefs, but she gained something she hadn't expected: the ability to see the bigger picture and find solutions incorporating more voices.

Debate Formats: Understanding the Game

Sports like basketball, soccer, and tennis have different rules, and debates have various formats. Here's a look at some of the most common ones:

1. Lincoln-Douglas Debate (LD)

❖ *Focus*: *Ethics, philosophy, and values.*
❖ *Structure*: *One-on-one debate, where each side argues for or against a resolution based on principles and moral reasoning.*
❖ *Timeframe*: *Each speaker takes turns presenting their case, rebutting, and making closing arguments.*

In this format, it is not just about facts—it is about why something is right or wrong at its core. This type of debate forces you to think about the *why* behind your beliefs.

2. Parliamentary Debate (Parli)

❖ *Focus*: *Speed, wit, and creativity.*
❖ *Structure*: *Two teams (usually two speakers per team) debate a resolution with limited preparation time.*
❖ *Twist*: *The topics are often revealed minutes before the debate begins, so you must think fast and rely on your instincts.*

This format feels like a mental race—it is fast fun and pushes you to trust your ability to adapt.

3. Public Forum Debate (PF)

❖ *Focus*: *Real-world, current issues.*
❖ *Structure*: *Two teams debate a resolution on a timely topic— like healthcare policies or international relations.*

Public forum debates are designed to appeal to a general audience, not just debate experts. It is like having a public conversation about issues that affect everyone, and your goal is to make your points accessible and transparent.

Rules That Keep Things Fair

While each format has its structure, some universal rules apply to almost every debate:

1. **Respect Your Opponent**: No interruptions, no insults, no sarcasm. Debate is about ideas, not personal attacks.
2. **Time Limits**: Each speaker has a set amount of time to present their argument, ask questions, and give rebuttals. Time management is key—if you run out of time, you can't make your point.
3. **Stick to the Topic**: Stay focused on the resolution you're debating. If you wander off-topic, the judges will notice, which can cost you points.

The Mindset of a Debater

Debate isn't just about being quick on your feet—it's about approaching discussions with curiosity and humility. The best debaters aren't the ones who scream, interrupt, or "win" by intimidation. They're the ones who stay calm, listen carefully, and respond thoughtfully.

Here's what makes a great debater:

❖ *Curiosity*: *Wanting to understand every angle of an issue.*
❖ *Empathy*: *Understanding your opponent's position, even if you disagree.*

❖ **Resilience**: *Staying calm and collected, even when the pressure is high.*

The Debate that Changed History

Let's return to the 1858 debates between Abraham Lincoln and Stephen Douglas. These debates weren't held in classrooms—they were political showdowns that drew massive crowds. People would travel miles and spend hours standing in the heat just to hear two men debate issues like slavery and states' rights.

What made these debates unforgettable wasn't just the words spoken—it was the way Lincoln and Douglas showed the power of reasoned argument. Lincoln, known for his calm and logical demeanor, didn't attack Douglas personally. Instead, he made his points with clarity and precision, turning complex issues into ideas that everyday people could understand.

This historical example shows that debate isn't just about sounding smart—it's about *connecting* with your audience.

Your First Debate Challenge

If you've never debated before, don't worry—you don't need a podium or an audience of hundreds to get started. Here's your first challenge:

1. Pick a topic you're passionate about (it could be anything—school dress codes, climate change, or the pros and cons of social media).

2. Write down three points supporting your argument and three *against* it. This exercise helps you see both sides of the issue.

3. Ask a friend or family member to take the opposing side and practice debating for five minutes.

Practicing both sides will sharpen your ability to think critically and respond thoughtfully.

Your Voice in the Debate World

Debate isn't about being the loudest person in the room— it's about being the most thoughtful. It's about using your voice not to overpower but to illuminate.

As you step into your first debate, remember: You don't have to win to grow. Each discussion is a chance to strengthen your mind, discover new perspectives, and become more confident and articulate.

Building a Persuasive Argument

Picture this: you're sitting in the audience at a school debate competition. Two students are presenting their arguments. The first student rattles off statistics like they're reading from a textbook. The second starts with a story about a real person affected by the issue, ties it to a more significant point and ends with a powerful call to action.

Who would you remember more?

That's the magic of a persuasive argument—it doesn't just give information; it moves people. Whether you're debating in front of an audience or simply trying to convince your parents to let you stay out past curfew, building a strong, persuasive argument is a skill that can change the way you communicate forever.

Why Some Arguments Fall Flat

Most people think persuasion is about piling up facts. But here's the truth: facts alone don't convince people. Emotions, stories, and credibility make the difference. You've probably been in conversations where someone presented all the correct statistics but didn't change anyone's mind. Why? Because persuasion isn't just about *what* you say—it's about *how* you make your audience feel.

If you've ever zoned out during a lecture filled with numbers and bullet points, you've experienced this firsthand. People remember arguments that touch their emotions, stir their imaginations, and connect with their values.

The Persuasion Formula: Ethos, Pathos, Logos

To build a persuasive argument, the ancient Greek philosopher Aristotle gave us a blueprint that still holds up today. The best arguments use a combination of the following:

1. **Ethos (Credibility)**: Why should the audience trust you?
   a. Are you knowledgeable? Do you seem honest and fair?
2. **Pathos (Emotion)**: How can you make the audience care?

a. Can you make them feel empathy, fear, hope, or pride?

3. **Logos (Logic)**: Is your argument logical and supported by facts?

a. Are your points clear, reasonable, and backed by evidence?

A tremendous persuasive argument doesn't rely solely on one of these—it weaves all three together.

The Story of Tyler: Turning the Tide

Tyler was running for student body president but wasn't the most popular kid in school. His opponent was charming, confident, and had a substantial social following. Tyler knew he couldn't out-charm his opponent, but he had something else: a vision.

During his campaign speech, Tyler didn't start with promises or slogans. Instead, he began with a story:

"Last year, I was sitting in the back row at the assembly, feeling invisible. I didn't think anyone noticed me—until the new school counselor stopped me in the hall and asked if I was okay. That small moment made me feel seen and changed my entire year. I'm running for student body president to ensure every student feels that way—seen, heard, and included."

The room went quiet. Students who usually tuned out leaned forward. Tyler then presented his plan—clear, actionable steps to create mentorship programs and student support groups. By the time he finished, the audience wasn't just listening—they were invested.

Tyler didn't win his election because of popularity; he won because his argument wasn't just logical but personal and emotional.

Step 1: Start with a Strong Premise

Your premise is the foundation of your argument—the main idea you're trying to prove. Think of it like the thesis of an essay or a company's mission statement. A strong premise is:

- ❖ *Transparent*: *Your audience shouldn't have to guess what your point is.*
- ❖ *Debatable*: *If everyone already agrees with your premise, it's not much of a debate.*
- ❖ *Meaningful*: *Your premise should matter to your audience. Why should they care?*

Let's look at an example:

Weak Premise: *School lunch should be healthier.*

Strong Premise: *Schools should adopt student-led menus to improve nutrition and prevent food waste.*

The second premise is stronger because it's specific, new, and has real-world implications.

Step 2: Support Your Premise with Evidence

Once you have your premise, you need evidence to support it. This is where *logos* come in—your logical points. Evidence can include:

- ❖ *Statistics*: *Numbers that show trends or facts.*

o *Example: "Over 60% of students surveyed said they skip school lunch because they don't like the options."*

❖ **Expert Opinions**: *Quotes or research from credible sources.*

o *Example: "According to a nutritionist who works with schools, balanced meals improve focus by 20%."*

❖ **Anecdotes**: *Personal or real-world stories that make your point relatable.*

o *Example: "In one high school that implemented student-led menus, food waste decreased by 40%."*

Step 3: Address Counterarguments

A persuasive argument isn't just about proving why you're right—it's about showing you've considered the other side. Addressing counterarguments makes you look thoughtful, not defensive.

Imagine you're arguing for student-led menus. A counterargument might be: *"But won't that take too much time and money?"* Instead of ignoring that point, acknowledge it and offer a solution:

"Organizing a student-led menu program will take effort, but schools can start small—by letting students vote on one new menu item per semester. This keeps costs low while giving students a voice."

Addressing concerns head-on strengthens your argument and builds trust with your audience.

Step 4: Create an Emotional Connection

Here's where *pathos* comes in—the emotional heartbeat of your argument. Think back to Tyler's story. He didn't just list reasons why he'd be a good leader—he made his audience *feel* his message.

To create an emotional connection:

❖ **Tell a Story**: *Share a personal experience or someone else's story that illustrates your point.*

❖ **Use Imagery**: *Paint a vivid picture with your words so your audience can see what you're describing.*

❖ **Speak with Empathy**: *Show that you care about the people affected by the issue.*

When you combine logic with emotion, your argument becomes persuasive and unforgettable.

Step 5: End with a Strong Call to Action

Don't leave your audience wondering, *What now?* End your argument with a clear call to action—a step they can take or a takeaway that stays with them.

Example:

❖ *"I'm not just asking you to vote for a new school menu. I'm asking you to be part of something bigger—an effort to make school lunches a source of pride, not leftovers."*

A powerful closing ties everything together and leaves your audience inspired, not just informed.

The Power of Persuasion in Real Life

Learning to build a persuasive argument doesn't just help you in debates—it helps you in life. Whether you're negotiating with a teacher, pitching an idea to your club, or convincing your parents to let you take a trip with friends, persuasion is everywhere.

The more you practice, the more you'll realize that being persuasive isn't about "winning"—communicating with clarity, purpose, and authenticity.

Your Persuasion Challenge

Pick a topic you care about and write a short argument using the steps in this chapter. Share it with a friend or family member and ask for feedback:

❖ *Was your premise clear?*
❖ *Did your evidence strengthen your point?*
❖ *Did your story create an emotional connection?*

The more you practice building persuasive arguments, the more confident you'll become—not just as a debater but as a communicator who can make your voice heard.

Rebuttals and the Art of Refuting Opposing Points

Imagine this: You're in the middle of a debate. Your opponent makes a point that sounds so convincing you can almost see the audience nodding in agreement. Your heart skips a beat. What do you do now? This is where the true magic of debate happens—not just in making your case but in your ability to respond, challenge, and strengthen your argument in real-time.

This is the art of the rebuttal—turning your opponent's strongest argument into your most significant advantage. But a rebuttal isn't about crushing someone with clever comebacks or overwhelming them with facts. It's about listening closely, thinking critically, and responding with clarity and respect.

The Story of Ava: Turning the Tables

Ava's debate topic was whether schools should switch to a four-day school week. She argued against the idea, but her opponent had just made a strong case about how an extra day off would help students recharge and pursue extracurricular passions. The audience seemed impressed, and Ava could feel the pressure building.

But Ava didn't panic. Instead, she smiled and said, *"My opponent makes a great point—rest is important. But here's the question: what happens when students use that extra day off to binge-watch shows instead of recharging? Studies show that students who lack structure during long weekends often feel more stressed when they return. So instead of solving burnout, this plan might make it worse."*

The crowd murmured in agreement. Ava acknowledged her opponent's point, reframed it, and strengthened her position. Her rebuttal wasn't just practical—it was memorable.

Why Rebuttals Matter

Rebuttals show that you're not just presenting your ideas in isolation but engaging with the conversation. A well-crafted rebuttal:

* ❖ *Demonstrates that you've listened carefully to the opposing side.*
* ❖ *It strengthens your credibility because you're addressing counterarguments head-on.*
* ❖ *Build trust with your audience by showing that you're fair and thoughtful, not dismissive, or defensive.*

The Key to a Great Rebuttal: Listening Like a Detective

Rebuttals aren't about preparing a comeback before your opponent finishes speaking. They're about listening. Imagine you're a detective searching for inconsistencies, unanswered questions, or assumptions that don't quite hold up.

Ask yourself:

* ❖ *What is their primary point?*
* ❖ *What assumptions are they making?*
* ❖ *Is there missing evidence?*
* ❖ *How does their argument affect real-world outcomes?*

The best rebuttals don't just challenge what was said—they dig deeper and reveal the complete picture.

The Anatomy of an Effective Rebuttal

A strong rebuttal has three main parts:

1. **Acknowledge the Opponent's Point**: Start by showing that you've heard and understood their argument. This makes you seem respectful and fair, not dismissive.
    a. Example: *"My opponent raises a valid concern about school safety."*
2. **Challenge or Reframe It**: Point out a flaw, assumption, or missing context in their argument.
    a. Example: *"However, focusing solely on metal detectors ignores other effective safety measures, such as mental health support and peer counseling."*
3. **Reinforce Your Argument**: Returning the conversation to your key message and explaining why your side is stronger.
    a. Example: *"By investing in community-building programs, schools can create safer, more supportive environments where issues are addressed before they escalate."*

Common Rebuttal Pitfalls (and How to Avoid Them)

1. **Attacking the Person Instead of the Idea**:
    a. *Mistake*: "You clearly don't understand how schools work."
    b. *Why It's Wrong*: Personal attacks make you lose credibility and can alienate your audience.

c. *Better Approach*: Focus on the idea, not the person.

d. Example: "The idea assumes that funding for these programs will always be available, but history shows that budgets fluctuate."

2. **Overloading with Too Many Points**:

a. *Mistake*: Listing five counterarguments at once.

b. *Why It's Wrong*: It overwhelms the audience and dilutes your message.

c. *Better Approach*: Focus on one or two key points addressing their argument's heart.

3. **Ignoring Valid Points**:

a. *Mistake*: Pretending your opponent's strong points don't exist.

b. *Why It's Wrong*: Your audience will notice and see you as evasive.

c. *Better Approach*: Acknowledge strong points and explain why your argument still holds.

d. Example: "While it's true that shorter school weeks may reduce burnout temporarily, the long-term impact on academic performance must be considered."

The Power of Confidence in Rebuttals

Confidence isn't about being the loudest person in the room—it's about staying calm, composed, and straightforward. A strong rebuttal doesn't need to be flashy or aggressive. A calm measured response often carries more weight because it shows opposing views do not rattle you.

Take a deep breath before you speak. Slow down your pace. Make eye contact with your audience. People are more likely to trust what you're saying when you talk with steady confidence.

How to Prepare for Rebuttals

Even though you can't predict every question or argument, you can still prepare by thinking ahead.

1. **Research Both Sides**: The best debaters know their opponent's arguments and their own. Spend time researching counterarguments, so you're not caught off guard.
2. **Practice "What-If" Scenarios**: Think of tough questions your opponent might ask and practice responding to them.
3. **Stay Focused on Your Core Message**: Always bring the conversation back to your main point, no matter how strong your opponent's argument is.

The Story of Marcus and the Unexpected Question

During a debate about social media regulations, Marcus was asked a question he hadn't anticipated: *"If you support social media guidelines, aren't you limiting free speech?"* For a second, he froze. The question felt more significant than the topic—it was about a fundamental right.

Instead of panicking, Marcus paused and said: *"That's a really important question, and I'm glad you asked. Free speech is a right we should all protect. But with that right comes responsibility. Social media companies already regulate certain harmful content to protect users. I'm arguing that we should expand those protections—not silence voices but create safer spaces where everyone can participate freely."*

The room was silent for a beat, and then the applause began. Marcus's calm, thoughtful answer didn't just defuse the question—it strengthened his position.

Your Rebuttal Challenge

This week, I practiced crafting rebuttals by choosing a controversial topic and writing down the strongest argument for the opposing side. Then, write out a respectful rebuttal that:

❖ *Acknowledges their point.*
❖ *Identifies a flaw, assumption, or missing context.*
❖ *Reinforce your key argument.*

Read it aloud and notice how your tone and delivery feel. Remember, your goal isn't to "win" by shutting someone down—it's to lead a conversation that strengthens your message and expands understanding.

Rebuttals as a Superpower

Learning to deliver strong rebuttals isn't just a debate skill—it's a life skill. Whether you're standing up for yourself in a disagreement, defending a project idea in a meeting, or explaining your point of view to someone with a different opinion, the ability to respond with clarity and respect can change the course of the conversation.

When you listen with curiosity, respond with confidence, and lead with respect, you don't just win debates—you win trust.

Building Resilience – Bouncing Back from Setbacks in Debate

It's the final round of the school debate competition. You've practiced for weeks, researched every angle, and rehearsed until you could recite your argument in your sleep. But as you walk off the stage after delivering your rebuttal, you notice something: the audience isn't clapping as enthusiastically as you'd hoped. Worse, your opponent's closing statement lands like a thunderclap, earning loud applause.

Your stomach sinks. The thought flashes through your mind: *I blew it.*

Setbacks like this can feel like the end of the world—especially when you've poured your heart into something. But what if I told you that setbacks aren't failures? They're some of the most potent teachers you'll ever have. Resilience isn't about never falling—it's about getting stronger every time you do.

The Story of Skylar: The Comeback Kid

Skylar had always been a natural speaker. She was the kind of person who could make people laugh, think, and cheer with just a few words. But during the semifinals of the regional debate tournament, everything fell apart.

She froze during her rebuttal. Her mind went blank, and instead of delivering her carefully crafted response, she muttered something vague, stumbled over her words, and sat down early. The silence in the room was deafening. She felt humiliated.

For days, Skylar avoided her teammates. She repeatedly replayed the moment in her head, thinking about what she should have said, wishing she could return in time. But then her coach called her and said something she would never forget, *"Skylar, the strongest people aren't the ones who never fall—they're the ones who get back up, no matter how many times they stumble."*

Skylar showed up to practice the next day. Instead of avoiding the moment where she froze, she leaned into it. She practiced recovering from mistakes—starting over mid-sentence, improvising when she forgot a line, and staying calm when things didn't go as planned. When the final tournament came, she didn't just win—she gave the speech of her life.

Her comeback wasn't about perfection—it was about resilience.

Why Resilience Matters

Life isn't a perfectly rehearsed script. It's unpredictable, messy, and full of surprises. Debate is the same way. No matter how much you prepare, there will be moments when things go off track—when someone challenges you with an unexpected argument, or you forget what you planned to say.

Resilience is what helps you handle those moments with grace instead of panic. It's the skill that allows you to pivot when things go wrong, adapt when circumstances change, and stay grounded when the pressure is high.

What Happens in Your Brain When You Fail

You should know that when you experience a setback, your brain doesn't just feel emotional pain—it reacts as if you've experienced a physical injury. The same part of your brain that processes a broken bone processes the sting of failure. That's why it feels so intense—it's not "just in your head."

But the good news is that your brain is also wired to grow stronger from failure. Every time you bounce back from a setback, your brain builds new connections that make you more resilient. You're training your mind to handle stress and setbacks more effectively.

The Resilience Formula: A.C.E.

To build resilience in debate (and in life), you can use the **A.C.E. Formula**:

1. **Acknowledge**:
   a. Recognize what happened and how you feel. Don't shove it aside or pretend it didn't matter.

Acknowledging your emotions helps you process them.

    b.   Example: "I felt embarrassed when I forgot my point. That's normal—it was a tough moment."

2. **Collect Your Thoughts**:

    a.   Instead of spiraling into negative self-talk (*"I'll never be good at this"*), collect yourself by asking: *What did I learn from this? What can I do differently next time?*

    b.   Example: "Next time, I'll build in a few moments to breathe and regroup if I lose my place."

3. **Engage and Try Again**:

    a.   The final step is to get back in the game. Resilience doesn't mean avoiding the things that scare you—it means facing them head-on.

The Power of Failure Stories

Think about some of the most inspiring leaders you've ever heard of—people like Michael Jordan, Oprah Winfrey, or J.K. Rowling. Every one of them faced devastating setbacks. Michael Jordan was cut from his high school basketball team. Oprah was told she wasn't fit for television. Twelve publishers rejected J.K. Rowling before *Harry Potter* became a global phenomenon.

What made them extraordinary wasn't their talent—it was their resilience. They didn't let failure define their story—they let it fuel their comeback.

How to Handle Real-Time Setbacks in Debate

In a debate, setbacks can happen in real-time. Here's how to recover when the unexpected happens:

1. **Pause, Don't Panic**: A pause isn't a sign of failure—it's a sign of composure. Taking a breath before responding shows your audience that you're thoughtful, not rattled.
2. **Acknowledge the Moment**: Call it out with humor or grace if something goes wrong.
   a. Example: "Well, that wasn't the smoothest transition, but let's get back on track!"
3. **Recenter Your Focus**: Instead of obsessing over the mistake, focus on your next point. Keep moving forward—your audience will follow your lead.

The Story of Ethan: Owning the Moment

Ethan was known for his quick wit and strong arguments. But during a citywide debate, he misquoted a statistic during his opening statement—and his opponent called him out on it.

The room went silent. Everyone expected Ethan to stumble, but he nodded and said, *"You're right. I got that number wrong. But the point I'm making still holds—here's why."* Then, he calmly backed up his argument with another piece of evidence.

Ethan's honesty didn't make him look weak—it made him look trustworthy. The judges didn't penalize him for the mistake; they rewarded him for his resilience and authenticity.

Resilience Outside of Debate

Resilience isn't just valuable for debate—it's a life skill. Whether you're facing a tough exam, a friendship challenge, or a personal disappointment, your ability to bounce back can change how you handle setbacks.

Here are some real-world situations where resilience matters:

- ❖ *In School*: *If you bomb a presentation or get a lower grade than expected, resilience helps you reflect, regroup, and improve.*
- ❖ *In Friendships*: *Misunderstandings and arguments happen. Resilience means staying open to communication and forgiveness instead of walking away.*
- ❖ *In Goals*: *When you don't make the team or club you were hoping for, resilience keeps you motivated to try again or pivot to new opportunities.*

Your Resilience Challenge

Think back to a time when you faced a setback. Write down:

1. What happened?
2. How you felt in the moment.
3. What you learned from the experience.
4. What did you (or could you do) to bounce back?

Then, set a small resilience goal for yourself—like speaking up in class after a rough presentation or trying out for something you didn't make the first time. Each time you face a setback and bounce back; you build a skill that will serve you for life.

Your Story Isn't Over

Remember: setbacks aren't endings—they're chapters in your story. What matters isn't whether you fall—it's how you rise.

Looking back on your journey, you won't remember every mistake or misstep. What you'll remember are the moments when you chose to keep going. And those are the moments that will make your story worth telling.

CHAPTER 4

DESIGN THINKING FOR PROBLEM-SOLVING

When you think of problem-solving, what comes to mind? Maybe it's solving a tricky math problem or figuring out how to fix a broken phone. But the truth is life's most critical problems—the ones that matter—don't come with clear instructions or a single correct answer. That's where design thinking comes in.

Design thinking isn't just about finding solutions—it's about understanding problems at a deep level, asking the right questions, and staying open to creative, unexpected answers. It's the approach companies like Apple use to design products they love. It's how community leaders address challenges like poverty, education, and access to healthcare. And yes, it's how you, too, can solve the issues that matter most to you—whether that's making your school more inclusive, addressing homelessness in your community, or leading a volunteer project.

But here's the cool part: design thinking isn't just for adults working at big companies. It's for teenagers, too. Creativity, empathy, and fresh perspective make you naturally great at it.

What Is Design Thinking Really?

Design thinking is a way of approaching problems with empathy, curiosity, and experimentation. At its core, it's about understanding the people affected by an issue, brainstorming ideas, testing those ideas, and learning from what works and what doesn't.

Unlike traditional problem-solving, which often jumps straight to "fixing" things, design thinking slows down the process so you can understand what's happening. It's less about being right and more about being curious.

Let's break it down step by step.

The Five Stages of Design Thinking
1. Empathize (Understand the People Affected)

Imagine trying to solve homelessness without ever talking to someone who's experienced it. You can't solve a problem if you don't understand what it feels like to live it. The empathy stage is about listening, observing, and putting yourself in someone else's shoes.

    a.   In Phoenix, for example, many assume that homelessness is caused solely by financial struggles. But when you listen to real stories, you learn that things like mental health, addiction, and even a lack of affordable housing play huge roles.

2. Define (Clarify the Problem)

Once you've gathered stories and data, the next step is defining the problem clearly. This doesn't mean listing everything wrong—it means focusing on the heart of the issue.

a. Instead of saying, "Homelessness is a problem," you might define it as: "Many young adults in Phoenix are unable to find affordable housing after aging out of foster care, leading to cycles of homelessness."

3. Ideate (Brainstorm Solutions)

Now comes the fun part—generating ideas. This stage is about being creative and thinking outside the box.

a. What if there were mentorship programs that connected young adults with host families?

b. What if abandoned buildings were converted into low-cost housing centers with built-in job training programs?

In this stage, you don't worry about whether your ideas are perfect. You write down everything—no matter how wild—because sometimes the craziest ideas spark the best solutions.

4. Prototype (Build a Small-Scale Version)

A prototype doesn't have to be fancy—it's a simple version of your solution that you can test.

a. For example, before launching a city-wide mentorship program, you could pilot it with five families and five young adults to see what works and what doesn't.

5. **Test (See What Works and Improve It)**

The final step is to test your prototype, get feedback, and make changes. In design thinking, testing isn't the end of the process—it's part of the process. Sometimes, your first idea won't work as expected, but that's okay. You'll learn, adapt, and get closer to a solution that truly works.

The Story of Mia and the Empty Field

Mia was a high school junior in Phoenix who walked past an empty, overgrown lot near her school daily. The lot had become where people threw their trash—old furniture, broken bikes, and food wrappers. Everyone complained about it, but no one did anything.

One day, Mia decided to use what she'd learned in her design-thinking club to tackle the problem. Instead of assuming the lot just needed to be cleaned up, she started with empathy. She interviewed neighbors, local shop owners, and even her classmates for two weeks. What she discovered was surprising: most people didn't just want the lot cleaned—they wanted it turned into something useful, like a garden or a gathering space.

With that knowledge, Mia and her friends defined their problem: *The lot isn't just an eyesore—it's a missed opportunity to unite the community.*

They brainstormed ideas and devised three prototypes: a small outdoor library, a pop-up garden with planter boxes, and a space for weekly farmer's markets. They tested each idea by inviting community members to try them out. The feedback was overwhelmingly positive. The city approved a permanent community garden and event space permit within six months.

Mia's success wasn't just about cleaning up the lot—it was about listening, engaging, and co-creating solutions with her community.

Why Teenagers Make Great Design Thinkers

1. **You Ask Big Questions**: Teenagers often see things adults overlook and ask, "Why can't this be better?" That curiosity is the heart of design thinking.
2. **You're Adaptable**: Unlike adults who sometimes get stuck in their ways, you're open to new ideas and willing to change direction when something doesn't work.
3. **You Care Deeply**: Whether it's about the environment, equality, or mental health, your generation is passionate about improving the world—passion fuels innovation.

Applying Design Thinking to Your Own Life

You don't have to tackle a city-wide issue to use design thinking. Here are a few ways you can apply it in everyday life:

❖ *Class Projects: Instead of guessing what your teacher wants, ask for feedback early and often to ensure your project meets expectations.*
❖ *Friendship Conflicts: Instead of assuming why someone is upset, have a conversation to understand their perspective before jumping to conclusions.*

❖ *Extracurricular Events*: *When planning a school event, interview your peers to find out what would make the event more fun and meaningful.*

Design Thinking and the Bigger Picture: Tackling Homelessness in Phoenix

Later in this chapter, we'll dive deeper into how design thinking can help address large-scale challenges like homelessness. You'll learn how to ask the right questions, identify root causes, and build solutions that aren't just quick fixes but meaningful changes.

Your Design Thinking Challenge

This week, choose one problem in your school or community—big or small—and apply the five stages of design thinking:

1. Empathize: Talk to at least three people affected by the issue.
2. Define: Write a clear, focused problem statement.
3. Ideate: Brainstorm at least ten possible solutions—no idea is too wild.
4. Prototype: Choose one idea and create a tiny miniature version (a drawing, a presentation, or even a physical model).
5. Test: Share your prototype with someone and get feedback.

By practicing design thinking, you're not just solving problems—you're developing a mindset that will help you create change wherever you go.

Design thinking teaches us that the best solutions don't come from trying to be the most thoughtful person in the room but from being the most empathetic and curious. When you take time to understand the people behind the problem, your solutions don't just fix things—they make lives better.

Understanding the Root Causes of Complex Problems

When you see a problem like homelessness, it's easy to assume that the solution is obvious: "Build more shelters" or "Provide job training programs." But the truth is, complex problems—like homelessness, inequality, or school bullying—are rarely caused by one thing, and they can't be solved with a single, quick fix.

Think of a tree. The branches and leaves are what you see above ground. But those branches are supported by something more profound—the roots. If the roots are weak or tangled, the tree won't thrive. The same is true for problems in our world. If you only focus on what you can see, you'll miss the deeper causes. Design thinking helps us dig deeper to find those "roots" so that our solutions address the real problem—not just the symptoms.

In this chapter, we'll explore how to identify the root causes of an issue and use real-world examples—including the challenge of homelessness in Phoenix—to show how robust this process can be.

The Story of Marcus and the Messy Cafeteria

At Marcus's high school, there was one thing everyone complained about: the cafeteria was a disaster after lunch. Tables were left sticky with spilled drinks, trays were piled high with trash, and the floor looked like a battlefield of dropped fries and crumpled napkins.

The school's administration tried everything—they hired extra custodians, put up posters that read: "Clean Up After Yourself!" and even added more trash cans. But nothing worked.

Then Marcus, a school leadership team member, decided to dig deeper. Instead of guessing why the cafeteria was such a mess, he started interviewing students. What he discovered surprised everyone:

❖ *Many students said they didn't have enough time to eat before the bell rang, so they rushed to class and left their trays behind.*
❖ *Others said the cafeteria line was so slow that they had only a few minutes to eat when they got their food.*

The real problem wasn't that students were lazy or disrespectful—the schedule and cafeteria flow made it almost impossible for them to clean up properly.

Marcus presented these findings to the administration, who adjusted the lunch schedule to give students more time and added a second food line to speed things up. Within weeks, the cafeteria was noticeably cleaner—not because of stricter rules, but because they addressed the underlying issues.

What Is Root Cause Analysis?

Root cause analysis is like being a detective for problems. Instead of stopping at the surface, you ask questions until you understand the "why" behind the problem. Here's how it works:

The "5 Whys" Technique

The "5 Whys" is a simple but powerful tool. You start with the problem, then ask "why" until you get to the root cause.

Example: Tackling Youth Homelessness in Phoenix

- ❖ **Problem**: *Many young adults in Phoenix are experiencing homelessness.*
- ❖ **1st Why**: *Why are they experiencing homelessness?*
    - o They can't afford rent.
- ❖ **2nd Why**: *Why can't they afford rent?*
    - o They don't have steady jobs.
- ❖ **3rd Why**: *Why don't they have steady jobs?*
    - o They lack the necessary skills or education.
- ❖ **4th Why**: *Why do they lack skills or education?*
    - o Many aged out of the foster care system without access to career support or mentorship.
- ❖ **5th Why**: *Why didn't they have access to mentorship?*
    - o There aren't enough transitional programs to support foster youth as they become independent adults.

By digging deeper, you uncover a critical insight: the root cause isn't just the cost of rent—it's the lack of transitional support for foster youth. With this understanding, your solutions will be more targeted and effective, like creating mentorship programs or career training centers tailored to young adults who have aged out of foster care.

The "Fishbone Diagram"

A fishbone diagram is another tool that helps you visualize the causes of a problem. Imagine a drawing of a fish skeleton:

❖ *The "head" is the problem you're trying to solve.*
❖ *The "bones" branching out from the spine represent different categories of causes (e.g. economic, social, systemic).*
❖ *Each smaller bone represents specific factors contributing to the issue.*

This method is beneficial when tackling significant, complicated problems because it helps you organize your thoughts and see connections you might've missed.

Case Study: Homelessness in Phoenix, AZ

Let's take a closer look at homelessness in Phoenix—a city that has faced rising housing costs and an increase in unsheltered individuals in recent years.

When most people think about homelessness, they picture someone who is out of work and can't pay rent. But homelessness has many faces:

❖ *Some people become homeless after a medical emergency wipes out their savings.*

❖ *Some struggle with untreated mental health conditions or addiction.*

❖ *Some veterans return home and can't find the support they need.*

❖ *Some, like foster youth, don't have family safety nets to fall back on.*

Each of these stories has its root causes; without understanding those causes, any solution will only scratch the surface.

For example, if the city only builds more shelters without addressing mental health care, addiction services, and job training, the cycle will continue. However, if city leaders work with affected individuals to understand their needs—offering mental health support alongside housing programs—they can create more lasting change.

Why Root Cause Analysis Changes Everything

When you identify the root cause of a problem, something powerful happens:

❖ *You stop wasting time and energy on band-aid solutions that only address symptoms.*

❖ *You start creating solutions that make a real, lasting impact.*

❖ *You build trust with the people you're trying to help because they see you care enough to understand their experience.*

Root cause analysis isn't just about solving problems—it's about changing how you approach challenges in every part of your life. Whether working on a group project, planning an event, or improving your relationships, understanding the "why" behind the issue can lead to breakthroughs.

The Story of Sophia: Asking the Right Questions

Sophia's club wanted to increase attendance at their annual community service event. In the past, attendance had been low, and most members assumed it was because people didn't care. But Sophia wasn't convinced. She decided to dig deeper.

She sent out an anonymous survey asking students why they hadn't attended in previous years. The results shocked her:

- ❖ *Many students said they didn't know about the event until it was too late.*
- ❖ *Others said they couldn't get transportation to the event location.*

With this information, Sophia's club made two key changes: they launched a month-long promotional campaign and organized carpools. The next event had double the turnout—not because they forced people to come, but because they removed the obstacles that had been in the way.

Your Root Cause Analysis Challenge

Choose a problem you care about—in your school, community, or life. Use the "5 Whys" technique or create a fishbone diagram to break it down. Ask yourself:

- ❖ *What's causing this issue?*

* *Are there patterns I didn't notice before?*
* *How can I address the deeper causes, not just the surface symptoms?*

By practicing root cause analysis, you'll become the leader who doesn't just solve problems—you transform them.

Learning to look past the surface and ask the right questions unlocks a new way of thinking. You'll see that even the biggest, messiest problems can be untangled if you're willing to dig deep, listen closely, and approach challenges with empathy and creativity.

Creative Ideation – Generating Solutions That Stick

Once you've identified the root cause of a problem, the next step is where things get exciting—it's time to brainstorm solutions. But this isn't just about coming up with a quick fix or choosing the most obvious idea. Creative ideation is about pushing your brain to think outside the box, generating ideas you never thought possible, and finding solutions that work and last.

Consider this step the "what if" stage, where you ask bold questions, imagine new possibilities, and let your creativity flow. The best ideas often come from unexpected places, so the goal is to be open, curious, and fearless.

The Story of Caleb's Community Garden

Caleb loved his neighborhood, but there was a problem: the local park was rundown, and no one used it anymore. The benches were broken, the grass was patchy, and the basketball court was cracked. The city council suggested adding more trash cans and repainting the benches, but Caleb felt that wouldn't bring people back.

So, he gathered a group of friends and brainstormed new ideas using design thinking. Instead of starting with fixes, they asked: *What would excite people to come here?* They spent an entire afternoon throwing out ideas—from pop-up food trucks to weekend concerts and community gardens.

One idea stuck: a garden where people could plant fruits and vegetables together. The group didn't know if it would work but decided to prototype it. They built a few small planter boxes in one corner of the park and invited neighbors to contribute. Within weeks, the garden became a neighborhood hit, and people who hadn't stepped foot in the park for years gathered there every weekend.

What made Caleb's idea work wasn't just that it was creative—it addressed the heart of the problem: the park wasn't just empty because it was rundown but because it didn't feel meaningful to the people who lived nearby.

Why Brainstorming Matters

At its core, brainstorming is about possibility. It's not about having "the right answer"—exploring every idea, no matter how wild or straightforward it may seem. Creative ideation helps you:

❖ *Get Unstuck: When you feel trapped by the exact old solutions, brainstorming helps you see new paths.*

❖ *Involve Others*: *The best ideas often come when you collaborate with people who think differently from you.*
❖ *Create Ownership*: *People feel invested in the solution when they contribute ideas.*

The Rules of Brainstorming

To make your brainstorming sessions effective, it's essential to set a few ground rules:

1. **No Judging**: This is a safe space for ideas—no matter how "out there" they seem. Judging ideas too early can shut down creativity.
2. **Quantity Over Quality**: At this stage, focus on generating as many ideas as possible. You can narrow them down later.
3. **Build on Each Other's Ideas**: Instead of dismissing an idea, consider ways to improve or expand it. Creativity is contagious!
4. **Stay Focused on the Problem**: While it's fun to come up with wild ideas, make sure they still address the root cause of the problem.

Creative Ideation Techniques

If you've ever sat in front of a blank page and thought, *I have no idea where to start,* don't worry—you're not alone. These brainstorming techniques can help spark your creativity:

1. **"Yes, And..."**
   a. This technique comes from improve comedy and is all about building momentum. Instead of saying

"no" to an idea or pointing out why it won't work, you add to it.

    b.   **Example:**

        i.   Friend 1: "What if we turned the empty lot into a pop-up art gallery?"

        ii.   Friend 2: "Yes, and we could invite local artists to host workshops."

        iii.   Friend 3: "Yes, and we could have live music to draw more people in."

2. Mind Mapping

    a.   Start with your main problem in the center of a page (like "school lunches are boring") and draw branches for related ideas (like "theme days," "student-chosen menus," or "guest chefs"). This visual approach helps you see connections and spot new ideas.

3. Role-Playing

    a.   Imagine you're someone affected by the problem—a student, a parent, a teacher—and brainstorm from their perspective. This helps you come up with ideas that are more empathetic and relevant.

The Power of Wild Ideas

Some of the best solutions often start as "wild" ideas during brainstorming. Think about some of the world's most innovative creations:

❖ *Post-it Notes: Originally an experiment that failed to create a strong adhesive revolutionized how we organize ideas.*

❖ *Ride-sharing apps: Who would've thought people would trust strangers to drive them around? Now, companies like Uber and Lyft are part of daily life.*

Wild ideas work because they break free from the usual patterns of thinking. They challenge assumptions and make you ask, *why not?*

From Ideas to Action: Choosing a Prototype

Once you've brainstormed a list of ideas, it's time to choose one to prototype. But how do you decide which idea to pursue? Here are a few questions to guide you:

1. **Does it Address the Root Cause?**
   a. Make sure the idea isn't just a quick fix—it should address the deeper issue you identified.
2. **Is It Feasible?**
   a. Can you build a miniature version of it with your resources?
3. **Does It Inspire People?**
   a. The best ideas don't just solve problems—they excite and engage others.

The Story of Ana and the After-School Program

Ana noticed that her school's after-school program had low attendance despite offering great activities like tutoring, art classes, and sports. Instead of assuming the program needed better advertising, Ana brainstormed with classmates.

One student suggested, *"What if we had a mascot who handed out flyers?"* Another added, *"Yes, and what if the mascot made funny TikTok videos about the program?"* Someone said, *"Yes, and what if we created a student spotlight where kids could share what they've learned at the program?"*

They first tested the mascot idea, which worked better than expected. Attendance increased, and the program became where students felt seen and celebrated. Ana's group didn't settle for ordinary solutions—they leaned into creativity, which paid off.

Your Creative Ideation Challenge

Choose a problem—big or small—and host a brainstorming session with friends or family. Use one of the techniques from this chapter (like "Yes, and..." or mind mapping) and write down every idea, no matter how wild. Then, narrow your list to one or two ideas you can prototype.

Remember: the goal isn't to develop the "perfect" idea—it's to explore possibilities, take risks, and have fun with the process.

Why Creativity Changes the Game

Creative ideation isn't just a step in the problem-solving process—it turns ordinary solutions into extraordinary ones. When you approach challenges with curiosity and imagination, you don't just solve problems—you change the story entirely.

So, the next time someone says, *"That's impossible,"* ask yourself: *What if it isn't?*

Prototyping – Turning Ideas into Reality

You've done the hard work: empathizing with those affected by the problem, defining the root cause, and brainstorming creative solutions. Now it's time for the exciting part—prototyping. This step is where ideas leave the drawing board and become something tangible. A prototype doesn't have to be perfect or flashy—it just needs to be honest enough for you to test and get feedback.

Think of prototyping as building a rough draft. Just like you wouldn't submit an essay without writing a draft and making revisions, you wouldn't roll out a big solution without testing a more petite version first. Prototyping helps you see what works, what doesn't, and what can be improved.

The Story of Maya's Mental Health Initiative

Maya's school had a growing problem: students were stressed, overwhelmed, and burned out, but they didn't feel comfortable talking about it. Maya and her friends knew something had to change but didn't know where to start. They brainstormed dozens of ideas—student-led support groups, mental health workshops, and a quiet "de-stress zone" in the library.

Instead of launching everything at once, they decided to prototype just one idea: "Mental Health Mondays"—a 10-minute guided mindfulness session during homeroom. The idea was simple but powerful.

In the first week, only a few teachers participated. But Maya's team collected feedback, adjusted, and created a short video explaining the benefits of mindfulness. By the third week, participation had doubled. The school made Mental Health Mondays a permanent schedule.

Maya's prototype wasn't perfect at first—but because she started small and stayed open to feedback, it grew into something meaningful.

Why Prototyping Matters

Prototyping helps you:

❖ *Test Ideas Before Committing: Instead of spending time and resources on a full-scale project, you can test a more petite version first.*

❖ *Learn Through Action: Prototypes give you real-world data—you learn what works and what doesn't by seeing your idea in action.*

❖ *Fail Safely: If something doesn't work, it's okay—you're testing, not launching. Each "failure" is just another step toward improvement.*

Types of Prototypes

Prototypes don't all look the same. Depending on your project, your prototype might be:

1. **A Physical Model**: If your idea is a product, build a simple version using paper, cardboard, or clay.

2. **A Digital Mockup**: If your idea involves technology (like a website or app), create a basic sketch or clickable demo.

3. **A Pilot Program**: If your idea is a service (like a mentorship program), start with a small group before expanding.

4. **A Role-Playing Scenario**: If your idea involves interactions (like conflict resolution training), act it out with friends and observe what works.

The key is to create something you can show, test, and improve.

The "Build-Measure-Learn" Cycle

Prototyping follows a cycle called "Build-Measure-Learn":

1. **Build**: Create your prototype—don't worry about making it perfect.

2. **Measure**: Test your prototype and collect feedback. What worked? What didn't? What surprised you?

3. **Learn**: Use the feedback to make changes and build a stronger version.

This process isn't a one-time thing—it's a loop. You might go through the cycle multiple times, refining your idea with each iteration.

The Story of Evan's Debate App

Evan was frustrated by how hard it was to get real-time feedback during debate practice. He proposed an app to let teammates leave quick notes during practice rounds, like "strong rebuttal" or "speed up here."

However, Evan didn't know how to code an app from scratch, so he created a paper version instead. He pointed out feedback sheets and handed them out during practice rounds. The sheets worked so well that a friend who knew coding helped him turn the concept into an essential app.

After testing the app with his team, Evan learned that some feedback categories were too broad, so he added more specific options. Eventually, the app became a tool for his team and debate clubs across the district.

What made Evan's prototype successful wasn't the technology—it was the feedback loop. He built, measured, learned, and improved until the app met the needs of its users.

How to Get Meaningful Feedback

To improve your prototype, you need honest, helpful feedback. However, not all feedback is created equal. Here's how to get the kind of feedback that makes your prototype stronger:

1. **Ask Specific Questions**: Instead of asking, "What do you think?" ask things like:
   a. "What did you like most?"
   b. "What felt confusing or unclear?"
   c. "What would you change?"
2. **Observe, Don't Just Ask**: Sometimes people can't put their feedback into words, but their actions tell you a lot.

Watch how they interact with your prototype—where do they hesitate or get stuck?

3. **Stay Open**: Feeling defensive when someone points out a flaw in your idea is expected. But remember, feedback isn't criticism—it's information that helps you grow.

From Prototype to Launch

You can launch your idea once you've refined your prototype through feedback. But even at this stage, it's essential to stay flexible. No solution is ever "finished"—there will always be room for improvement as you learn more and adapt to new challenges.

The Story of Jordan's Community Mentorship Program

Jordan had a vision: to create a mentorship program for teens who wanted to pursue careers in STEM (science, technology, engineering, and math). But instead of starting with a full-scale launch, she decided to prototype it with just five mentor-mentee pairs.

In the first round, Jordan learned that some mentors didn't have enough time to meet in person, so she added virtual meetings as an option. She also found that mentees felt more engaged when they had small goals to work toward each month, so she created a "goal tracker" to keep everyone on track.

Because Jordan took the time to prototype and adjust, her mentorship program grew steadily—and the mentees weren't just learning STEM skills; they were gaining confidence and forming lasting connections.

Your Prototyping Challenge

This week, choose one of your ideas and create a simple prototype. It doesn't have to be perfect—it just needs to be honest enough to test. Share it with someone you trust and ask for feedback.

Remember: prototypes aren't about proving your idea is perfect—they're about learning and growing. Each version brings you one step closer to a solution that works.

Why Prototyping Empowers You

When you prototype, you're not just dreaming—you're building. You're bringing an idea from your imagination into the real world, where it can make a difference. And that's what makes prototyping so powerful—it shows you that change doesn't happen far away in boardrooms or government offices.

Change starts with you.

Testing and Iterating – Making Good Ideas Even Better

Congratulations—you've built your prototype and shared it with the world. But here's the thing: the first version of your idea is rarely perfect. It's *not supposed* to be perfect. This is where one of the most critical steps in design thinking comes in: testing and iterating.

Testing isn't about proving that your idea is flawless—it's about discovering what works, what doesn't, and how to improve it. Iteration is making small, thoughtful changes based on feedback until your solution meets the needs of the people it's meant to help.

The Story of Leo's Literacy Project

Leo was passionate about helping younger students improve their reading skills. His idea was to create a buddy system where older students read with younger ones for 30 minutes daily. He prototyped his concept by starting with five buddy pairs and testing it for a week.

The feedback came in quickly:

❖ *The younger students loved having reading buddies but sometimes got distracted after 15 minutes.*
❖ *Some older students felt unsure about how to help when a younger buddy struggled with a tricky word.*

Instead of scrapping his idea, Leo iterated. He shortened the reading sessions to 20 minutes and gave older students a simple guide that included encouragement tips and strategies for helping with difficult words.

Leo's literacy program became a hit after two more rounds of testing and feedback. By the end of the semester, 80% of the younger students had improved their reading comprehension by at least one grade level.

Leo's success didn't come from getting everything right the first time—it came from his willingness to learn, adapt, and improve.

Why Testing and Iterating Matter

When you skip the testing phase, you risk launching something that doesn't quite work—or worse, something that unintentionally worsens the problem. Testing and iterating allow you to:

❖ *Catch Issues Early: Small mistakes are more manageable (and cheaper) to fix than big ones.*

❖ *Involve the Community: Testing invites feedback from the people affected by the problem, making your solution more meaningful and inclusive.*

❖ *Build Confidence: When you see your idea improving over time, you gain the confidence to take on more significant challenges.*

How to Run a Successful Test

Testing isn't just about asking, *"Do you like this?"* It's about creating opportunities to observe how people interact with your solution and gathering actionable feedback.

Here's a step-by-step guide to running a successful test:

1. **Set Clear Goals**
    a. What do you want to learn from this test? Are you trying to determine if your solution is easy to use, effective, or engaging?

b. Example: *"We want to see if younger students stay focused during the 20-minute reading session."*

2. **Create a Feedback Plan**

a. Decide how you'll gather feedback. Will you observe participants, use surveys, or conduct interviews?

b. Example: *"We'll ask the younger students how they felt during the session and observe how often they get distracted."*

3. **Stay Open to Surprises**

a. Testing often reveals things you didn't expect— sometimes things that have nothing to do with your original goals. Be open to what you learn, even if it's not what you expected.

The "Iterate, Don't Agitate" Mindset

When you receive feedback, it's easy to get defensive. After all, this is your idea—you've poured your time and energy into it. But remember feedback isn't personal—it's a gift that helps you grow.

Instead of thinking, *"They didn't like my idea,"* try thinking, *"They showed me how to improve my idea."*

Great innovators—from inventors to entrepreneurs— succeed because they see feedback as fuel, not failure.

Iteration in Action: The Story of Emma's Social Media Campaign

Emma was part of her school's environmental club, and her team wanted to run a social media campaign to promote sustainable habits, like using reusable water bottles and cutting down on single-use plastics.

Their prototype was a series of infographic posts with facts and statistics about plastic pollution. But when they tested the posts, they noticed something: people were scrolling past them without engaging.

Instead of getting discouraged, Emma's team decided to iterate. They swapped out the infographics for short videos featuring students showing their eco-friendly habits—like decorating reusable water bottles or packing lunches in reusable containers.

The results were terrific. Engagement tripled, and students started tagging their friends and sharing their sustainable tips. Emma's team learned that their audience connected more with personal stories than abstract facts—and that insight made all the difference.

The Iteration Cycle

Iteration isn't a one-time fix—it's an ongoing cycle. Here's how it works:

1. **Test**: Share your prototype with users and observe how they interact.

2. **Get Feedback**: Gather feedback to understand what worked, what didn't, and why.
3. **Make Changes**: Use the feedback to make minor, focused improvements.
4. **Repeat**: Run another test with the updated prototype and gather more feedback.

Each time you go through the cycle, your solution becomes more substantial and more aligned with the needs of the people it serves.

The Story of Phoenix's Homeless Outreach Initiative

In Phoenix, a local organization launched a mobile outreach program to connect unsheltered individuals with resources like housing support, mental health care, and job assistance. Their prototype was a mobile van that offered on-the-spot assistance.

During their initial tests, the team realized that many individuals hesitated to approach the van because they associated it with law enforcement. Instead of scrapping the program, the team iterated. They partnered with community members known and trusted by unsheltered individuals, and those volunteers became the "bridge" between the van and the community.

The program's new approach increased participation by 60%—not because the initial idea was terrible, but because the team was willing to adapt based on feedback.

Your Testing and Iteration Challenge

Take the prototype you created in the last chapter and test it with at least one person. Use the feedback to make at least one meaningful change, then test again. Ask yourself:

❖ *What surprised me during the test?*
❖ *What feedback was most helpful?*
❖ *What change had the most significant impact?*

Why Testing and Iterating Make You a Stronger Leader

Testing and iterating teach you something valuable: perfection isn't the goal—progress is. When you embrace feedback, stay curious, and make continuous improvements, you become a leader who's not afraid of change but empowered by it.

You don't have to get it right the first time. The most impactful solutions in history—from the lightbulb to the smartphone—resulted from countless iterations.

So, as you move forward with your ideas, remember every test, tweak, and adjustment brings you one step closer to making a real difference.

CHAPTER 5

BUILDING EMOTIONAL

INTELLIGENCE

Imagine walking into the cafeteria and seeing someone sitting alone, their head down, picking at their food. Most people might glance, feel bad for a second, and move on. But what if you didn't? What if you sat down, asked how they were doing, and listened? That simple act—reaching out with empathy—can change someone's entire day.

Emotional intelligence (EI) is the ability to understand and manage your own emotions while being aware of and considerate of the feelings of others. It's the foundation of outstanding leadership—not just because it makes you kinder, but because it helps you connect, inspire, and lead in a way others want to follow.

Why Emotional Intelligence Matters More Than You Think

You're taught how to solve math problems, write essays, and memorize historical facts. But life's school challenges—navigating friendships, working on a group project, or dealing with failure—require a different skill set. That's where emotional intelligence comes in.

The ability to regulate your emotions, show empathy, and communicate clearly can mean the difference between making a problem worse and building a stronger connection. Research even shows that emotional intelligence is a better predictor of success in life than IQ.

The Story of Saesha: Changing the Atmosphere with Kindness

Saesha was the type of student who noticed the little things—when someone seemed overwhelmed during group projects or when a classmate was unusually quiet. She didn't see herself as a leader in the traditional sense—she wasn't the loudest or the most outgoing. But Saesha's quiet leadership was rooted in emotional intelligence.

One day, during a Model UN meeting, one of the newer students, Chloe, broke down in tears after struggling to present her research. The room fell silent, and no one knew what to do. But Saesha calmly approached Chloe, handed her a water bottle, and said, *"Take your time—we're here to support you."*

She didn't rush Chloe or try to "fix" the situation. She simply gave Chloe the space to breathe and feel safe. A few minutes later, Chloe started again—and nailed her presentation.

After the meeting, Chloe told Saesha, *"I would've quit if it weren't for you."*

Saesha's emotional intelligence didn't just help Chloe—it transformed the whole group. People began checking in with each other more, encouraging and supporting one another's efforts.

The Four Core Components of Emotional Intelligence

Emotional intelligence isn't something you're born with or without—it's a skill you can practice and strengthen. Let's break down the four main components:

1. **Self-Awareness**
   a. Self-awareness is the ability to understand your emotions and recognize how they affect your thoughts and actions.
   b. When you're self-aware, you can catch yourself before you snap at someone when you're stressed or pause before making a rash decision.

2. **Self-Regulation**
   a. Self-regulation is about managing your emotions, especially in challenging situations. It doesn't mean suppressing how you feel—it means responding in a way that aligns with your values.
   b. Instead of yelling when you're frustrated, you take a breath and express your feelings calmly.

3. **Empathy**
   a. Empathy is the ability to understand and share the feelings of others. It's about listening, paying attention, and showing that you care.
   b. When you're empathetic, you can sense when someone needs support, even if they're not saying it outright.

4. **Social Skills**
   a. Social skills are about communication, building relationships, and resolving conflicts. Leaders with strong social skills know how to inspire and bring people together.

The Science Behind Emotional Intelligence

Here's something amazing: your brain has something called neurons—special brain cells that fire when you experience emotion and see someone else experiencing it. That's why you can "feel" someone's sadness or excitement just by watching them.

This means empathy isn't just a nice idea—it's wired into your biology. And the more you practice empathy and self-awareness, the stronger these neural pathways become.

The Story of Jason: Learning Self-Regulation

Jason was known for being intelligent but impulsive. He often jumped into arguments during debates, cutting people off and raising his voice when he felt passionate about a point. His ideas were good, but his delivery was harsh, alienating his teammates.

One day, after a heated meeting where things went off the rails, his coach pulled him aside and said, *"Jason, your ideas are strong, but your emotions are steering the ship. What would happen if you paused before speaking?"*

Jason didn't like hearing it at first—it felt like criticism. But he decided to give it a try. At the next meeting, when he felt the familiar rush of frustration, he paused, took a deep breath, and asked, *"Can I clarify something before we move forward?"*

The difference was night and day. Instead of an argument, the discussion became a productive conversation. By the end of the meeting, Jason's teammates were nodding along instead of tuning out.

Jason's ability to self-regulate didn't just make him a better debater—it made him a better leader.

Why Empathy Is a Superpower

Empathy isn't just about being nice—it's about creating connections that build trust and respect. Here's what happens when you lead with empathy:

- ❖ *People feel heard and valued.*
- ❖ *Teams work better because they feel safe to share ideas and take risks.*
- ❖ *Conflicts are resolved more quickly because you address the emotions behind the disagreement, not just the facts.*

How to Strengthen Your Emotional Intelligence

1. **Pause and Reflect**: When you're feeling overwhelmed or upset, take a moment to check in with yourself. What are you feeling, and why?
2. **Practice Active Listening**: When someone is speaking, focus entirely on their words—not on what you're going to say next.

3. **Ask Open-Ended Questions**: Instead of offering advice immediately, ask questions like, *"How did that make you feel?"* or *"What do you need right now?"*

4. **Name Your Emotions**: Instead of saying, "I'm fine" when you're not, try naming what you feel—like frustration, excitement, or disappointment. Naming your emotions helps you process them more effectively.

5. **Celebrate Small Wins**: Emotional growth doesn't happen overnight. Celebrate moments when you handle a challenging situation with calm, empathy, or resilience.

The Ripple Effect of Emotional Intelligence

When you lead with emotional intelligence, the impact extends beyond you. Just like Saesha's small act of kindness changed the atmosphere of her Model UN group, your empathy and self-awareness can influence the people around you in unexpected ways.

Think about the leaders you admire. Chances are, they aren't just innovative or successful—they make you feel seen, respected, and inspired. That's the power of emotional intelligence. It's not about being perfect—it's about showing up with authenticity and care.

Your Emotional Intelligence Challenge

This week, practice one of the four components of emotional intelligence:

❖ *Start a journal to reflect on your emotions and triggers.*

❖ *Listen to someone without interrupting or offering advice—just be present.*

❖ *Notice a moment when you're about to react impulsively and pause before responding.*

Your Story Matters

The most influential leaders in history—from Martin Luther King Jr. to Malala Yousafzai—weren't just known for their ideas. They were known for their empathy, resilience, and ability to connect with people on a deeper level.

Your ability to lead with emotional intelligence can be a game-changer—not just for the people around you, but for yourself. When you understand your emotions and lead with empathy, you're not just solving problems but building bridges that change lives.

Self-Management – Staying Calm and Focused Under Pressure

Imagine you're in the middle of a big moment—a debate final, a soccer championship, or a class presentation. Your heart is pounding, your palms are sweaty, and your mind feels like it's racing a million miles an hour. Suddenly, the pressure feels overwhelming.

What do you do?

Do you let panic take over, or do you take a deep breath and stay calm? This ability—to manage yourself even when the stakes are high—is called **self-management**, and it's one of the most important skills you can develop as a leader.

Self-management isn't about ignoring your emotions or pretending you're fine when you're not. It's about recognizing your feelings, staying grounded, and making thoughtful choices instead of reacting impulsively. The secret weapon helps great leaders navigate challenging situations confidently and clearly.

The Story of Savar: Leading with Calm Under Pressure

Savar was known for his quick thinking and calm demeanor, but even he wasn't immune to pressure. During the state robotics competition, his team spent weeks perfecting their presentation and coding their robot. Everything was running smoothly—until it wasn't.

Minutes before their final demo, their robot malfunctioned. It wouldn't respond to commands, and the screen flashed error messages. His teammates started to panic. One of them muttered, *"We're done. This is over."*

But Savar didn't flinch. He raised his hand and said, *"Take a breath. We've practiced too hard to give up now."* He calmly directed the team to run their backup program while he troubleshot the issue. Even though their robot didn't function perfectly during the demo, Savar's leadership under pressure impressed the judges more than the malfunction had hurt their score.

Ultimately, the team won the "Innovation in Engineering" award—not because their presentation was flawless, but because Savar's composure showed authentic leadership.

Why Self-Management Matters

In moments of stress, your brain's "fight or flight" response kicks in. This ancient survival instinct helped our ancestors escape danger, but it's not always helpful during a group presentation or difficult conversation. When stress takes over, thinking about problems or communicating calmly becomes harder.

Self-management when stress takes over gives you the tools to override that instinct and regain control. Here's why it matters:

- ❖ *Improves Decision-Making: When you stay calm, you can make thoughtful decisions instead of impulsive ones.*
- ❖ *Builds Trust: People are more likely to follow leaders who remain steady during the chaos.*
- ❖ *Increases Confidence: The more you practice self-management, the more confident you become in handling pressure.*

What's Happening in Your Brain Under Pressure

When stressed, your brain releases adrenaline and cortisol—hormones that prepare your body to react. Your heart beats faster, your breathing quickens, and your muscles tense up. This is your body's way of saying, *"Get ready—something important is happening!"*

But if you don't manage this response, your mind can go into overdrive, making it harder to focus or stay calm. You can train your brain to handle pressure by practicing mindfulness, breathing exercises, and reframing your thoughts.

Self-Management Techniques for Staying Calm and Focused

Here are some strategies that can help you strengthen your self-management skills:

1. **The Power of the Pause**
   a. When you feel yourself getting overwhelmed, take a moment to pause. A deep breath can give you enough time to slow down and reset.
   b. *Example*: During a class debate, if you forget your point, pause for a second and take a sip of water instead of rushing to fill the silence.

2. **Reframe the Situation**
   a. Instead of thinking, *"I'm failing,"* try reframing your thoughts to something more empowering, like, *"This is a chance to show resilience."*

3. **Visualization**
   a. Picture yourself succeeding before you even start. Professional athletes often visualize winning a game or nailing a performance—and you can do the same.

4. **The 4-7-8 Breathing Technique**
   a. Inhale for 4 seconds, hold your breath for 7 seconds and exhale for 8 seconds. This simple exercise can

calm your nervous system and help you regain focus.

5. **Set Small Goals in High-Pressure Moments**

   a. When everything feels overwhelming, break it down into smaller steps. Instead of considering the entire presentation, focus on the first slide or 30 seconds.

The Story of Emily's First Debate

Emily was new to the debate team and had never spoken to a large audience. The moment she stepped up to the podium, she froze. Her notes felt blurry in her hands, and her voice caught in her throat.

Then she remembered something Savar had told the team during practice, *"When you freeze, don't run—breathe."*

Emily took a slow, deep breath, met the eyes of one friendly face in the audience, and started again. Instead of rushing through her speech, she focused on speaking slowly and clearly. By the time she reached her closing statement, she wasn't just calm—she was confident.

After the debate, her teammates congratulated her. One said, *"You didn't just survive—you crushed it."*

Why Self-Management Makes You a Better Leader

The best leaders aren't the ones who never feel stressed—they're the ones who know how to manage it. When you can stay calm under pressure, you:

❖ *Inspire confidence in others.*

❖ *Navigate setbacks without falling apart.*

❖ *Make thoughtful decisions that keep things moving forward.*

Whether leading a group project, organizing a community event, or stepping into a leadership role at school, your ability to manage yourself sets the tone for everyone around you.

From Self-Management to Self-Mastery

Self-management isn't just a skill you use during big moments—it's something you can practice every day:

1. **Morning Check-Ins**: Start your day by asking yourself, *"What's my focus today? How can I approach challenges calmly?"*

2. **Daily Reflection**: At the end of the day, reflect on moments when you handled stress well and when you didn't. What can you learn from each experience?

3. **Celebrate Progress**: Self-management is a journey, not a destination. Celebrate the moments when you stayed calm and collected—it reinforces your growth.

Your Self-Management Challenge

Think of a situation where you often feel stressed or overwhelmed—projects or sports competitions. This week, try one self-management strategy when you feel the pressure rising. Pay attention to how it feels and what changes.

For an added challenge, share your experience with someone you trust, like a teammate, teacher, or family member. Sometimes, just talking about our progress helps you feel more empowered.

Why It's Okay to Feel Nervous (And Why That Can Be a Strength)

Here's a secret: feeling nervous isn't a weakness—it's a sign that you care. Even the best leaders, athletes, and performers get nervous. The difference is that they've learned how to use that energy as fuel instead of fear.

The next time you feel your heart racing before a big moment, remind yourself: *This is my brain gearing up for something important.* Then, take a deep breath, trust your preparation, and confidently step into your moment.

Self-management doesn't mean you'll never feel stressed— you'll know how to handle it when you do. When you practice staying calm, focused, and intentional, you don't just become a more decisive leader—you can thrive in any situation, no matter how challenging.

Empathy in Action – Understanding and Supporting Others

Empathy is one of the most powerful tools you can develop—not just as a leader, but as a human being. Empathy allows you to see the world from someone else's perspective, to feel what they're feeling, and to respond with kindness and understanding.

It's the difference between saying, *"That's not my problem,"* and asking, *"How can I help?"*

In a world where conversations often feel like competition, empathy reminds us that connection matters more than being "right." True leaders don't just guide people—they uplift them. And empathy is how they do it.

The Story of Vyom: Bringing a Team Together Through Understanding

Vyom wasn't the loudest person in the room. He wasn't the first to speak up during team meetings or the type to take over a group discussion. But Vyom had a quiet superpower—he knew how to listen.

During his sophomore year, Vyom was chosen to lead his school's science fair committee. The team was comprised of students with big ideas and even more prominent personalities. From day one, tensions were high. Some students wanted to focus on sustainability projects, while others insisted on high-tech robotics. Arguments broke out, and deadlines were slipping.

Most people would've tried to take control or force a compromise, but Vyom took a different approach. He invited each team member to share their thoughts—not in front of the whole group, but one-on-one. Instead of jumping in with solutions, Vyom listened. He asked questions like:

❖ *"Why is this project so important to you?"*
❖ *"What challenges do you see?"*

❖ *"How do you think we can meet in the middle?"*

As he listened, Vyom realized something surprising: the students weren't fighting because they didn't care—they were fighting because they cared *too much.* Everyone was so passionate about their ideas that they felt unheard.

At the next meeting, Vyom shared what he'd learned: *"We all want this science fair to be incredible, but that means we have to trust each other and collaborate."* He proposed a new plan: the team would divide into two groups—one focused on sustainability, the other on robotics—but they would work together on the fair's presentation and storytelling.

The result? The science fair was a huge success. Not only did the projects stand out, but the teamwork did, too. Teachers and students alike noticed how cohesive and supportive the committee was. One teacher said, *"I've never seen a group this organized and respectful."*

Vyom's empathy didn't just solve the conflict—it strengthened the team's bond.

What Empathy Is (And What It Isn't)

Empathy is often misunderstood. It's not about feeling sorry for someone or trying to fix their problems. Empathy is about:

❖ *Seeing someone's experience from their point of view.*
❖ *Listening without judgment or interruption.*
❖ *Responding in a way that shows you care.*

Empathy isn't about having all the answers but being present. Sometimes, knowing someone is willing to listen can make all the difference.

Why Empathy Matters in Leadership

Think about the leaders you admire most. Chances are, they aren't just innovative or successful—they make others feel seen and heard. Here's why empathy is a game-changer for leaders:

1. **Builds Trust**: When people know you care, they're more likely to trust and follow you.
2. **Strengthens Teams**: Empathy creates a sense of belonging and safety, which leads to better collaboration and innovation.
3. **Improves Problem-Solving**: When you understand different perspectives, you're better equipped to find solutions that work for everyone.
4. **De-escalates Conflicts**: Empathy helps you address the emotions behind disagreements, making it easier to find common ground.

The Science of Empathy

Your brain has mirror neurons—special cells that activate when you see someone else's emotions. That's why you might feel sad when you see someone cry or excited when your friend shares good news. Empathy isn't just an abstract idea—it's something your brain is wired to do.

But like any skill, empathy can be strengthened with practice. The more you actively listen, put yourself in someone else's shoes, and respond with care, the more natural empathy becomes.

The Story of Olivia and the New Kid

Olivia was one of the most popular students in her grade. She was friendly, funny, and involved in almost every school event. But one day, a new student, Ethan, joined her class, and he immediately became the target of teasing. He was shy, wore glasses that kept slipping down his nose, and always seemed to sit alone.

Most people ignored Ethan—or worse, joined in on the teasing. But Olivia couldn't shake the feeling that something wasn't right. Instead of brushing it off, she decided to sit next to him at lunch and discuss. At first, Ethan barely spoke. But Olivia kept showing up, asking questions, and sharing stories.

Slowly, Ethan began to open up. He told Olivia he'd moved schools five times in three years because his family struggled financially. He felt like he didn't belong anywhere. Olivia listened without interrupting, and instead of offering advice, she simply said, *"That sounds hard. I'm glad you're here."*

Within a few weeks, Ethan wasn't sitting alone anymore. He started making friends, joining clubs, and participating in school events. Olivia's empathy didn't just make Ethan feel welcome—it helped him find a sense of belonging.

How to Practice Empathy in Everyday Life

1. **Listen Without Distractions**: When someone is speaking, put away your phone, make eye contact, and focus entirely on their words.

2. **Ask Open-Ended Questions**: Instead of asking questions that can be answered with "yes" or "no," ask things like, *"How did that make you feel?"* or *"What was the hardest part for you?"*

3. **Acknowledge, Don't Minimize**: Instead of saying, *"It's not a big deal,"* try saying, *"That sounds tough—I'm here if you want to talk more."*

4. **Imagine Their Perspective**: Think about what it would feel like to be in their situation. What would you need in that moment?

Your Empathy Challenge

This week, I'm looking for an opportunity to practice empathy. Whether it's a friend going through something difficult or a classmate who seems distant, try to connect by listening and being present. You don't need the perfect words or solutions—just show that you care.

Why Empathy Creates Lasting Change

Empathy may seem small, but it can have a ripple effect. Like Vyom's ability to listen transformed his team, your empathy can create positive change in ways you can't always predict. When people feel heard and understood, they're more likely to extend that kindness to others.

Empathy can build bridges where there were once walls. And when you lead with empathy, you're not just in a world that often feels divided, making life better for others—you're shaping yourself into a leader who leaves an unforgettable impact.

Social Skills – Building Strong Connections and Inspiring Others

Think back to when you felt truly connected to someone—a friend who always understood your jokes, a teammate who had your back, or even a teacher who listened without judgment. Those moments weren't random; they happened because of strong social skills.

Social skills are the secret ingredient that helps you navigate friendships, lead group projects, and build communities where people feel valued and heard. But they're not just about being popular or extroverted—they're about knowing how to communicate, collaborate, and inspire. Whether you're a quiet thinker or a natural talker, mastering social skills can make you a leader people trust and respect.

The Story of Deepti: Uniting a Divided Group

Deepti wasn't the loudest person on the student council, but she had a unique gift—she knew how to bring people together. During her junior year, the council faced a crisis. The school had received funding for a significant event, and the group was supposed to decide whether to host a formal gala or a community festival. The room was divided in half, with both sides refusing to compromise. Meetings dragged on for weeks without progress, and tensions ran high.

Instead of picking a side, Deepti focused on the people, not the problem. After the meeting, she pulled aside the loudest voice and said, *"Can you tell me why this event is so important to you?"* One student wanted a gala because they believed the school needed something formal to build pride. Another wanted a festival because they wanted to include more students who couldn't afford a formal ticket.

Deepti didn't try to solve the problem immediately. She just listened. Once everyone felt heard, Deepti proposed something new: a combined event. The gala would kick off the weekend with an elegant dinner, but the following day would feature a festival open to everyone.

It was a risky idea, but the council agreed because Deepti had built trust and listened to the council. The event was so successful that the school made it an annual tradition. Deepti's social skills—her ability to listen, mediate, and find common ground—didn't just solve a disagreement. They created something lasting.

Why Social Skills Matter

Great leaders don't lead in isolation—they build connections. Whether you're leading a school club, organizing a volunteer event, or simply working on a group project, strong social skills can:

- ❖ **Strengthen Teamwork**: *When people feel heard, they're more likely to collaborate.*
- ❖ **Resolve Conflicts**: *Socially skilled leaders address misunderstandings before they become full-blown arguments.*
- ❖ **Inspire Trust**: *The ability to communicate openly and kindly builds credibility.*
- ❖ **Create Inclusivity**: *When you connect with different types of people, you create spaces where everyone feels welcome.*

The Science of Connection

Human beings are wired for connection. Studies show that when we feel a sense of belonging, our brains release oxytocin, which fosters trust and closeness. But the connection isn't just about small talk or hanging out—it's built on empathy, active listening, and authenticity.

The Story of Lucas and the Debate Team

Lucas was known for being sharp, quick-witted, and persuasive. But when he became captain of the debate team, things didn't go as smoothly as he expected. His natural confidence sometimes came off as dismissive, and some newer members felt intimidated. Instead of asking for feedback, Lucas assumed everyone was fine—until one of his best teammates quit, saying, *"This doesn't feel like a team anymore."*

That moment was a wake-up call for Lucas. He realized that leading wasn't just about winning arguments but building a team where everyone felt respected and valued.

Lucas changed his approach. Before diving into practice rounds, he started team meetings by asking how everyone felt. He encouraged quieter members to share their thoughts and made a point to praise people's improvements, not just their wins. Slowly, the atmosphere shifted. By the end of the season, the team wasn't just performing better—they trusted each other.

The Power of Listening

The most underrated social skill isn't speaking—it's listening. When you listen with your full attention, you show people that their words matter. Here's how to practice active listening:

1. **Put Away Distractions**: When someone is talking, put your phone down and make eye contact.
2. **Repeat Key Points**: After someone shares, say something like, *"So, what I'm hearing is..."* to show that you're engaged and understand.
3. **Ask Questions**: Instead of jumping in with your opinion, ask open-ended questions like, *"What do you think we should do next?"* or *"How did that make you feel?"*

The Role of Social Skills in Leadership

Social skills don't just help you in friendships—they're critical for leadership. Here's why:

1. **Building Team Spirit**: Whether leading a club or managing a group project, your social skills set the tone. Leaders who show kindness and respect create teams where people feel safe to share ideas.
2. **Dealing with Setbacks**: When things go wrong, strong social skills help you address concerns and keep morale high.
3. **Influencing Without Authority**: Sometimes, leadership isn't about having a title—it's about earning respect. Socially skilled leaders inspire people to follow them, even when not "in charge."

The Story of Saesha and the Community Service Project

Saesha's school was organizing a food drive, and she was asked to lead the project. At first, Saesha felt overwhelmed—how was she supposed to motivate hundreds of students to donate when so many were busy with exams and sports?

Instead of pushing people with long announcements or guilt-tripping, Saesha took a different approach. She visited each homeroom and shared a personal story about volunteering with her family at a local shelter during the holidays. She talked about how small actions—like donating a single can of food—could make a big difference. She ended with, *"We're not just collecting cans. We're showing people in our community that they're not forgotten."*

Her speech wasn't flashy, but it was authentic. Students felt her sincerity, and donations poured in. Saesha's social skills—her ability to connect, inspire, and communicate her "why"—made the food drive one of the most successful events the school had ever held.

How to Strengthen Your Social Skills

1. **Practice Empathy**: Try to see things from someone else's perspective before reacting.
2. **Learn to Read the Room**: Pay attention to body language and tone—sometimes, people's emotions speak louder than words.
3. **Speak with Purpose**: Instead of speaking just to fill the silence, think about what message you want to share and how you want it to be received.
4. **Celebrate Others**: Recognize people's contributions, big or small. A simple *"Great job!"* or *"That was a fantastic idea"* can boost morale.

Your Social Skills Challenge

This week, focus on building stronger connections in one area of your life—with a classmate, a teammate, or a family member. Practice active listening, ask thoughtful questions, and show appreciation for their efforts.

For an added challenge, reflect on how those interactions made you feel. Did you notice a difference in how people responded?

Why Social Skills Create Lasting Impact

Leaders who master social skills don't just lead—they create communities. Like Deepti and Saesha, their ability to connect with others and build trust leaves a lasting impression. People remember how you make them feel, and when you lead with empathy, clarity, and respect, you create a legacy of connection and belonging.

Social skills aren't about popularity—they're about purpose. When you use your voice to include others, resolve conflicts, and bring people together, you don't just become a leader—you become someone others look to for guidance, even in the most challenging moments.

CHAPTER 6
GOAL SETTING AND TIME MANAGEMENT

Think about a moment when you felt excited about something—a big idea, a personal challenge, or a dream that seemed just within reach. Maybe it was trying out for the school musical, starting a fundraiser, or earning a spot on the varsity team. That first rush of excitement feels like pure energy. But what happens when the excitement fades and you're left with the hard work?

This is where so many people lose their way—not because they lack talent, but because they lack a plan. Goal setting isn't just about having a dream; it's about creating a step-by-step path to get there. It's the difference between looking at a mountain and feeling overwhelmed versus taking one steady step at a time and realizing you're capable of more than you imagined.

The Story of Logan's Leap

Logan loved photography. He spent hours experimenting with his dad's old camera, capturing sunrises, shadows, and candid moments of his friends. One day, he saw a flyer for the "Future Creators Art Exhibit" at the community center. The theme was "Moments That Matter." Logan's heart raced—this was his shot to highlight his work.

But as soon as he started planning, doubt crept in. What if his photos weren't good enough? What if no one even noticed them? Logan's excitement turned into anxiety, and he almost talked himself out of entering. But then his older sister gave him a notebook and said, *"Write it down. Write your goal and then break it into pieces."*

Logan did precisely that. He wrote:

1. **Choose five photo themes by Friday.**
2. **Shoot new photos on Saturday and Sunday.**
3. **Edit pictures the following week.**
4. **Print and frame by the submission deadline.**

With each step checked off, Logan felt more in control and less overwhelmed. On the day of the exhibit, his framed photo of a grandmother braiding her granddaughter's hair drew a crowd. People were moved by how it captured something simple yet universal. Logan didn't just take a picture—he told a story. And it all started with writing down his goal.

Why Goal Setting Works

When you write down your goals and create a plan, something incredible happens:

❖ *You shift from "wishing" to "doing."*
❖ *You gain clarity. Instead of feeling lost in a sea of tasks, you know exactly what to focus on.*
❖ *You stay motivated. Every small accomplishment builds momentum.*

❖ *You build resilience. Even when setbacks happen, a clear goal helps you get back on track.*

Dreams vs. Goals

A dream is saying, *"I want to be on the track team."*

A goal is saying, *"I'll practice running three miles every morning for four weeks."*

Dreams inspire you, but goals get you moving. The two work together. Without goals, dreams stay distant. Without dreams, goals can feel empty. When you connect your dreams to your goals, you create a purpose.

The SMART Method

To make your goals actionable, try using the SMART method. SMART goals are:

1. **Specific**: Be clear about what you want to achieve.
   a. *Vague*: "I want to get better at math."
   b. *Specific*: "I will improve my algebra grade by practicing 10 problems daily."
2. **Measurable**: Track your progress.
   a. Ask yourself: How will I know when I've succeeded?
3. **Achievable**: Be realistic but ambitious.
   a. Set goals that challenge you but aren't impossible.
4. **Relevant**: Make sure your goal aligns with your bigger picture.

a.   Example: If you dream of joining the robotics team, set a goal to learn coding basics.

5.   **Time-Bound**: Give yourself a deadline.

a.   Instead of saying, *"I'll read more,"* say, *"I'll finish this book by the end of the month."*

The Story of Grace's Gratitude Journal

Grace had always felt a bit scattered. Between her AP classes, soccer practice, and family responsibilities, she thought she juggled too many things at once. Her stress levels skyrocketed, and she often felt she was letting people down.

One day, her history teacher introduced the class to micro-goals—small, manageable actions that build momentum. Inspired, Grace set a micro-goal: to write in a gratitude journal for just two minutes every night. It seemed almost too simple at first, but within a week, she noticed something. Writing three small things she was grateful for helped her stay calm and focused, even during stressful days.

With that small success, Grace started applying micro-goals to her study routine and soccer practice. She didn't just survive her busy schedule—she thrived.

Why Some Goals Fail (And How to Avoid It)

Even with the best intentions, some goals fall apart. Here's why and how you can avoid it:

1.   **Too Vague**:

a.   *Problem*: "Get good grades" is unclear.

b. *Solution*: Be specific. *"Study for 30 minutes each night and review note every Sunday."*

2. **Too Overwhelming**:
   a. *Problem*: Big goals can feel impossible.
   b. *Solution*: Break it into smaller tasks. Instead of saying, *"Finish the science project,"* say, *"Research this week, outline next week, and build the model in the final week."*

3. **No Accountability**:
   a. *Problem*: It's easy to let goals slide if no one knows about them.
   b. *Solution*: Share your goals with someone who can check in with you.

The Story of Noah and the Talent Show Audition

Noah had always loved music but had never performed in front of a large audience. When his school announced its annual talent show, he hesitated. The thought of standing on stage terrified him. But deep down, he wanted to share his passion.

Noah set a goal: to prepare one song and audition in two weeks. Instead of practicing alone, he asked his best friend to listen and give feedback. Each day, Noah practiced one verse at a time, focusing on his timing and breathing. On audition day, his nerves didn't magically disappear, but he felt ready because he'd prepared in small, he felt ready.

Noah didn't win first place, but he earned a standing ovation and gained something more valuable: the confidence to step outside his comfort zone.

How to Stick to Your Goals

1. **Visualize Your Success**: Close your eyes and imagine how you'll feel when you reach your goal. Visualization can motivate you to push through challenging moments.
2. **Track Your Progress**: Use a planner, an app, or sticky notes to track small wins.
3. **Celebrate Milestones**: Treat yourself when you hit key points along the way.
4. **Stay Flexible**: Life happens. If something doesn't go as planned, adjust your timeline instead of giving up.

The Power of Purpose

Goals aren't just about productivity—they're about becoming the person you want to be. Every time you set and achieve a goal, you strengthen your resilience, confidence, and sense of direction. You prove to yourself that you can make things happen.

Think about the leaders, athletes, and artists you admire. None of them became successful overnight. Their achievements were built on small, consistent steps toward a bigger dream. The same is true for you.

Your Goal-Setting Challenge

Pick one goal you've considered: finishing a book, learning a new skill, or improving your grades. Write it down using the SMART framework. Then, create a plan with weekly tasks. Share your goal with someone you trust and ask them to check-in.

Real goals start with small steps. The key isn't perfection—it's progress.

When you set a clear goal and create a plan, you're not just hoping for success—you're building it, one step at a time. Whether your goal is personal, academic, or community-focused, every step forward brings you closer to the person you're meant to become.

Goal Setting – How to Create a Plan That Works

Imagine you're standing at the starting line of a race. The finish line looks so far away that you're already doubting yourself before taking your first step. But what if you concentrate on getting to the next checkpoint instead of focusing on the whole race? What if you broke the race down into manageable parts and gave yourself a chance to succeed, one small win at a time?

That's what goal setting is—it's not about jumping from start to finish in one giant leap. It's about building a path you can walk step-by-step. It's about dreaming big but acting small and steady.

The Moment When Big Things Start Small

Let me tell you about Ryan, a high school junior who dreamed of earning a full scholarship to a prestigious college. His dream wasn't about chasing prestige—it was personal. Ryan's mom worked two jobs, and he wanted to ease the financial burden on his family.

Ryan's teachers and friends knew he was bright but struggled with time management and consistency. One day, a mentor told him, *"Big dreams are reached with small goals. Build your future like a house—one brick at a time."*

That evening, Ryan wrote his dream at the top of a blank page: *"Full scholarship."* Then, he listed every step he'd need to reach that goal:

❖ *Improve SAT scores*
❖ *Strengthen his leadership experience*
❖ *Complete college applications early*

He broke down each of those steps even further. Instead of saying, *"Study for the SAT,"* he wrote: *"Study vocabulary for 20 minutes every weekday at 4p.m."* Instead of *"Volunteer more,"* he set a goal: *"Lead a food drive next semester with my local youth group."*

The result wasn't overnight magic—it was slow, steady progress. However, when Ryan checked off a small goal, he felt unstoppable. By senior year, Ryan didn't just meet his dream; he exceeded it—earnings multiple scholarships and becoming a student leader at his chosen university.

Why Goal Setting Changes Everything

When you set goals, you do more than just make a plan—you give yourself a sense of direction. Here's why goal setting works:

❖ **Priority***: You know exactly what you're working toward and why it matters.*
❖ **Prevents Overwhelm***: Breaking goals into smaller tasks helps you focus without feeling buried under pressure.*

❖ ***Increases Motivation***: *Small wins release dopamine in your brain, giving you bursts of confidence and joy.*
❖ ***Builds Resilience***: *When setbacks happen, having a plan makes adapting easier than giving up.*

Dream vs. Goal: What's the Difference?

❖ *A dream says, "I hope I get into college."*
❖ *A goal says, "I will write and revise my statement by October 1."*

Dreams inspire you, but goals move you forward. Without dreams, life lacks vision. Without goals, dreams stay out of reach. But when you align your dreams with actionable goals, you build something powerful momentum.

How to Build "SMART" Goals

One way to make your goals more effective is using the SMART framework. This method helps you create goals that aren't just ambitious and achievable.

1. **Specific**: Make your goals crystal clear
   a. *Vague*: "I want to get better at writing."
   b. *Specific*: "I will practice writing two monthly essays for the next three months."
2. **Measurable**: Create a way to track your progress.
   a. Example: "I will complete three chapters of my reading by Sunday."
3. **Achievable**: Make your goal challenging but realistic.

a. You can aim high—but break the goal into smaller, realistic milestones.

4. **Relevant**: Make sure your goals align with your overall dreams and values.

a. Example: If you want to become a lawyer, set goals that build skills like public speaking and critical thinking.

5. **Time-Bound**: Set deadlines to keep yourself accountable.

a. Instead of saying, *"I'll improve my grades,"* say, *"I will increase my GPA by next semester by dedicating one hour daily to studying."*

The Story of Chloe and the Marathon Mindset

Chloe's goal wasn't academic—it was athletic. She wanted to run a marathon in honor of her late grandfather, who had inspired her love of long-distance running. But the thought of running 26.2 miles was overwhelming. She doubted her stamina and wasn't sure how to prepare.

Chloe's coach told her, *"Don't focus on the full marathon— focus on the next mile."* So, Chloe broke the race down into smaller weekly goals:

❖ *Week 1: Run 2 miles without stopping.*
❖ *Week 3: Increase to 4 miles at a steady pace.*
❖ *Week 6: Add uphill sprints to build endurance.*

By race day, Chloe wasn't just ready—she was excited. She crossed the finish line with tears, not just because she finished the race but because she'd learned to believe in herself.

Why Some Goals Fail (And How to Avoid It)

Even with a great plan, some goals can fall apart. Here's why—and how you can avoid those pitfalls:

1. **Setting Goals That Are Too Broad**
   a. *Problem*: Saying, "I'll get better at science" doesn't give you a starting point.
   b. *Solution*: Make it actionable— *"I'll spend 30 minutes after school reviewing notes from today's lesson."*

2. **Lack of Accountability**
   a. *Problem*: If no one knows your goal, letting yourself slide is easier
   b. *Solution*: Share your goals with someone you trust—a friend, coach, or family member—who can check in and encourage you.

3. **All-Or-Nothing Thinking**
   a. *Problem*: One bad day can make you feel like you've failed.
   b. Instead of giving up, adjust your approach and keep going. Progress isn't linear—it's a journey.

How to Stick to Your Goals

1. **Visualize Your Success**: Imagine how you'll feel once you reach your goal. Visualization can strengthen your focus and motivation.

2. **Track Your Progress**: In a planner, an app, or a calendar, seeing your progress keeps you motivated.

3. **Celebrate Small Wins**: Don't wait for the final result to celebrate—recognize the little victories along the way.

4. **Stay Flexible**: Life is unpredictable. If your original plan doesn't work, adjust your timeline or approach instead of abandoning the goal entirely.

The Power of Writing Down Your Goals

Studies show that people who write down their goals are 42% more likely to achieve them. Why? Because writing makes your intentions tangible—it's like committing to yourself.

Take a blank sheet of paper or open a notes app. Write down one big dream, then break it and split it. Watch how something that once felt impossible becomes manageable.

Your Goal-Setting Challenge

Think about one dream you've been holding onto—whether it's personal or work it into a SMART goal and create a timeline with clear steps.

For an extra challenge, share your goal with a friend or mentor and ask them to hold you accountable. Celebrate each step you complete and remind yourself that progress—not perfection—is the goal.

Why Goal Setting Builds Leaders

Great leaders, athletes, and changemakers don't succeed by accident—they succeed because they've learned how to set clear goals and adapt when things get hard. You don't need to be complicated perfectly. You just need to keep moving forward.

By practicing goal setting now, you're not just preparing for the challenges you face today—you're building a foundation for the future. When setbacks come (and they will), your goals will be the compass that guides you back to your path.

Take your first step. Write it down. Because with every small action, you're getting closer to the person you're meant to be.

Time Management – Balancing Academics, Activities, and Life

Time can feel like sand slipping through your fingers—especially when balancing homework, sports, family, and social life. There are days when 24 hours just don't seem like enough. You have a history quiz to study for, a soccer game in the evening, a club meeting after school, and you promised your younger sibling you'd help with their science project.

Sound familiar?

But here's the thing: time isn't something you can control—it's something you can manage. The secret to feeling less overwhelmed isn't about magically creating more hours in the day—it's about being intentional with your time.

The Story of Ira: The "All-In" Overachiever

Ira was the definition of "all-in." She was the captain of the debate team, played the violin in the school orchestra, and volunteered at a local food pantry every weekend. Her planner looked like a jigsaw puzzle with every hour crammed with commitments.

At first, Ira thrived on adrenaline. But after a few months, the cracks started to show. She'd stay up late finishing homework, lose sleep over upcoming tournaments, and snap at her friends when overwhelmed. One day, she forgot her entire debate script for a big competition. She stood at the podium, mind blank, while the judges silently waited.

That moment was a wake-up call. Ira realized she couldn't keep running on empty. She needed to rethink how she spent her time—not by doing less, but by doing things smarter.

The Reset: How Ira Took Back Control

Ira's debate coach sat her down and said, *"You can't be at your best if you're burning out."* Together, they created a time management strategy that changed everything:

1. **The "Big Rocks" Method**: The coach told Ira to picture a jar. If you fill it with small pebbles first—like social media scrolling, distractions, and unnecessary tasks—you won't have room for the big rocks—your most important priorities. But if you put the big rocks in first, everything else falls into place.

Ira identified her "big rocks"—schoolwork, debate prep, and orchestra—and scheduled those first. Then, she fit smaller tasks around them, like texting friends or organizing her room.

2. **The "Two-Hour Focus Rule"**: Ira dedicated two uninterrupted hours each evening to her top priority. She turned off her phone instead of multitasking, closed extra tabs, and dived into one task at a time.

3. **The Art of Saying No**: This was the hardest part. Ira had to learn that saying no to specific opportunities wasn't failure but self-preservation. By choosing quality over quantity, she excelled at the things that mattered most.

Why Time Management Is a Superpower

When you manage your time well, you:

❖ *Feel More in Control*: *Instead of being pulled in a million directions, you purposefully guide your day.*

❖ *Reduce Stress*: *Clear priorities make it easier to avoid unnecessary worry.*

❖ *Build Consistency*: *Small, intentional habits lead to significant results over time.*

Time management isn't about squeezing every second dry—it's about aligning your time with what matters most to you.

The Story of Samira: The Procrastinator's Turnaround

Samira had a different problem. She wasn't juggling too many things—pushing everything to the last minute. Her motto was *"I work better under pressure,"* but the truth was, she didn't. She spent more time dreading her tasks than actually doing them.

When her teacher assigned a three-week group project, Samira's group begged her to stay on schedule. But Samira still fell into old habits—waiting until two days before the due date to start her part. She pulled an all-nighter, turned in a rushed presentation, and felt a pit in her stomach when she saw the final grade: a C-.

Samira felt terrible—not just because of the grade, but because she let her teammates down. One of them said, *"We needed you to step up."* It wasn't just a bad grade—it was a missed opportunity to show up as a leader.

Samira's Turnaround Plan

After that project, Samira made a promise to herself: no more waiting until the last minute. Here's how she changed her approach:

1. **The "15-Minute Rule"**: Samira set a timer for just 15 minutes whenever she didn't feel like starting. Once the timer was up, she could stop if she wanted—but she found herself in the flow most of the time and kept going.
2. **Chunking Big Tasks**: Instead of staring at the massive project and feeling overwhelmed, Samira broke it into smaller tasks—like "research three articles" or "create one slide."
3. **Rewarding Progress**: She gave herself small rewards, like a break to watch her favorite show after completing a section. This kept her motivated without feeling burned out.

Why Procrastination Happens (And How to Beat It)

Procrastination isn't about laziness—it's about fear or avoidance. Sometimes, tasks feel so big or intimidating that your brain convinces you to delay them. Here's how to overcome that:

- **Start Small**: Start with a tiny piece instead of tackling the whole assignment. Even writing one sentence can kickstart momentum.
- **Set Clear Deadlines**: Break the task into mini deadlines. For example, finish research by Friday, outline by Monday, and complete the draft by Thursday.
- **Remove Distractions**: Turn off notifications, find a quiet space, and set a timer for focus time.

Time Management Techniques That Work

1. **The Pomodoro Technique**:
   a. Work for 25 minutes, take a 5-minute break and repeat. After four cycles, take a more extended break.
2. **Time Blocking**:
   a. Schedule specific tasks during specific time slots in your day.
3. **The "Done List"**:
   a. Keep a list of what you've completed; instead, keep a list of what you've achieved. Seeing your progress builds momentum.

The Power of Prioritization

Think of your time like a playlist. If you only add random songs, you'll skip and shuffle all day. But if you build your playlist with intention, you'll create a flow that energizes you.

Ask yourself:

❖ *What are my "big rocks" today?*
❖ *What tasks can wait or be delegated?*

When you focus on your priorities instead of trying to do everything at once, you get more done and enjoy the process more.

Your Time Management Challenge

Choose one time management strategy this week—time blocking, the Pomodoro Technique, or the 15-minute rule. Reflect on how it changes your workflow and stress levels.

Write down your daily priorities each morning and review your nightly progress.

Why Time Management Builds Strong Leaders

Strong leaders don't just react to the chaos around them; they plan purposefully. By managing your time, you show yourself and others that you respect your commitments and well-being.

Time management isn't about being perfect—it's about being present. When you learn how to balance your priorities, you create space for the things that matter most: your growth, passions, and relationships.

Prioritization – Learning What Matters Most

Life is like a juggling act. You're balancing school, friendships, family, activities, and dreams. Some days, it feels like you barely keep everything in the air. But here's the truth: not all the balls you juggle are the same. Some are made of rubber—if you drop them, they'll bounce back. Others are made of glass—if you drop those, they can shatter.

Learning to prioritize means knowing which "balls" you can afford to drop and which you need to hold onto tightly. It's not about doing everything—it's about doing the right things.

The Story of Yuvraj: The Overachiever's Wake-Up Call

Yuvraj was the kind of person who said yes to everything. School clubs? Yes. Soccer practice? Yes. Helping a friend with a group project? Of course, yes. Yuvraj loved being involved and thrived on the feeling of being needed. But the constant yeses came at a cost—he was spread so thin that he felt like he was failing at everything.

One Friday afternoon, Yuvraj's history teacher returned an essay he'd rushed to finish at 2 a.m. the night before. A bright red "D+" glared back at him. Yuvraj's stomach sank. He had always been proud of his work, and this wasn't just a low grade—it felt like proof that he was falling apart.

That evening, Yuvraj's mom noticed his stress and asked, *"What's going on?"* Yuvraj admitted that he felt like he was drowning in commitments. His mom gave him a quiet nod and said, *"You're trying to be everything for everyone. But what do you want to be for yourself?"*

Yuvraj sat with that question for days. Slowly, he realized that while he loved being involved, he wasn't giving his energy to the things that mattered most to him. He was saying yes out of obligation, not passion.

The Power of Prioritization

Yuvraj decided to make some changes. He wrote down all his commitments and asked himself three questions for each one:

1. *Does this align with my goals?*
2. *Does this bring me joy?*
3. *Is this something I must do, or am I pressured to do it?*

He realized that some of his activities—like tutoring, which he'd taken on because he felt guilty saying no—didn't align with his goals or passions. Meanwhile, he felt alive during soccer practice and when working on science club projects.

So, Yuvraj made a tough but necessary decision: he scaled back his commitments and focused on what mattered most. He quit the tutoring job and cut back on extra club meetings. At first, he felt uneasy—what if people thought he was selfish? But instead of feeling guilty, Yuvraj found something unexpected: relief.

Within weeks, his grades improved, his energy returned, and he excelled in the things that mattered to him.

What Prioritization Means

Prioritization isn't about doing less—it's about doing the right things. When you prioritize, you make intentional choices about how to spend your time and energy. You learn to distinguish between what's urgent and what's important. Here's the key difference:

❖ *Urgent: Needs immediate attention (like replying to a last-minute email).*
❖ *Vital: Contributes to your long-term growth and well-being (like studying for an upcoming test or spending time with family).*

Sometimes, urgent things distract you from important ones. Prioritization helps you stay focused on the most significant goal of your future.

The Science of Overcommitment

Studies show that when juggling too many tasks, your brain's cognitive load can lead to burnout, decision fatigue, and reduced performance. The more things you try to focus on at once, the more your productivity drops.

But here's the good news: your brain loves clarity. When you give it a clear list of priorities, your stress levels drop, and your focus improves.

The Story of Mia and the Art of Saying No

Mia was the type of friend who never wanted to let anyone down. When classmates needed help, she was the first to volunteer. But as her schedule filled up, she stayed up late every night to finish her homework. She was exhausted.

One afternoon, Mia hesitated when her debate coach asked her to take on yet another lesson. She didn't want to seem ungrateful or unhelpful, but knew she'd burn out entirely. If she kept, she'd burn out completely.

So, Mia tried something different. She said, *"I appreciate the opportunity, but I'm at full capacity. I want to give 100% to what I'm already committed to."*

To Mia's surprise, her coach didn't get upset—instead, they nodded and said, *"Thank you for being honest."*

That small "no" was a turning point for Mia. She realized that setting boundaries didn't make her less of a leader—it made her stronger o

How to Prioritize Like a Pro

1. **Write It Down**: When you feel overwhelmed, list everything you need to do. Sometimes seeing it all on paper helps you organize your thoughts.
2. **Use the "Three-Task Rule"**: Focus on your top three priorities to accomplish those and consider it a win.
3. **Rank Your Tasks**: Label your tasks as "must do," "should do," and "nice to do." Focus on the "must-dos" first.

4. **Check In with Yourself**: Ask yourself weekly: *"Am I spending time on things that matter to me?"*

Your Prioritization Challenge

This week, I chose one day to practice prioritization. Write down everything you have to do and rank each task by importance. Focus on your top three tasks and see how they change your day.

For an added challenge, practice saying no to one request that doesn't align with your goals. Notice how it feels to protect your time and energy.

Why Prioritization Builds Strong Leaders

Strong leaders don't just fill their schedules—they protect their time for what matters most. They know that by saying no to distractions, they're saying yes to their purpose.

When you learn to prioritize, you take control of your time instead of letting your time control you. You build a life that aligns with your values, goals, and passions—and that's the foundation of authentic leadership.

Take a breath. Look at your commitments. Choose what matters. When you do, you'll find that you're not just juggling—thriving.

CHAPTER 7

SELF-DISCIPLINE BUILDING
THE HABITS THAT SHAPE
YOUR FUTURE

Self-discipline. It's not exactly a flashy word. You won't see it trending on social media or hear people chanting it at pep rallies. But here's the thing: self-discipline is the quiet force behind every great achievement. It's the difference between daydreaming about your goals and reaching them. It's what pushes you to keep going when the excitement fades, and the work gets hard.

Think of self-discipline as the foundation of a skyscraper. You don't see it when standing at the top admiring the view, but the building would collapse. In the same way, your habits— without that solid foundation and the daily choices you make—are the invisible structures that hold your future together.

The Story of Maya: The 5:00 AM Challenge

Maya had one goal: to make her high school's varsity swim team. But the competition was fierce, and the current varsity swimmers were fast—like *Olympic-level* fast. Her coach told her she needed to improve her stamina and technique if she wanted a real shot.

Maya knew what that meant—early morning practices, extra drills, and long hours at the pool. But there was one problem:

Maya loved to sleep in. The thought of waking up at 5:00 AM to jump into freezing water sounded like torture.

One night, as she lay in bed scrolling through her phone, she watched an interview with an athlete who said something that stuck with her: *"You don't need to be the best right away. You just need to show up."*

The following day, Maya set her alarm for 5:00 AM. When it went off, her mind screamed, *"Just five more minutes!"* But instead of giving in, she sat up, swung her legs over the side of the bed, and got up. It wasn't pretty—her eyes were half-closed, and her hair looked like a bird's nest—but she showed up.

Day after day, Maya dragged herself to the pool before sunrise. The more she showed up, the easier it got. And one day, something incredible happened: she beat her best time in practice. The following week, she did it again.

By the end of the season, Maya didn't just make the varsity team—she became one of their top swimmers. Self-discipline didn't just help Maya improve her skills—it changed how she saw herself. She wasn't just someone who *wanted* to be great. She was someone who *worked* for it.

Why Self-Discipline Matters

Self-discipline isn't about being perfect or never taking a break. It's about building habits that support your long-term goals, even when motivation fades. Here's why self-discipline is a game-changer:

1. **It Builds Resilience**: When you push through discomfort, you train your brain to handle challenges without giving up.
2. **It Creates Momentum**: The more you show up, the more progress you make, and the easier it gets to keep going.
3. **It Strengthens Self-Trust**: Every time you follow through on a commitment, you prove to yourself that you're reliable and capable.

The Science of Habits

Your brain loves habits because they save energy. Once something becomes a habit—like brushing your teeth or tying your shoes—you can do it almost automatically. But building new habits takes effort. It's like carving a new trail through the woods—the more you walk that path, the clearer it becomes.

The Story of Jordan's Social Media Detox

Jordan was addicted to his phone. He wasn't proud of it, but he couldn't help himself. Any free moment—between classes, at lunch, before bed—was spent scrolling through TikTok or replying to DMs. His screen time report showed an average of six hours a day, yet he constantly complained that he didn't have enough time to finish his homework or start the passion project he'd been discussing for months.

Jordan's sister challenged him: *"If you're serious about your goals, prove it. Put your phone away for just one hour a day and see what happens."*

Jordan resisted at first. What if he missed something important? But after some thought, he agreed to try it for one week. He set his phone on airplane mode for one hour every afternoon and worked on his project.

The first few days felt strange. He kept reaching for his phone out of habit. But by the end of the week, something changed. He realized how much more focused and productive he was without constant distractions. His one-hour detox turned into two, and soon, he found himself logging off social media earlier every night without even thinking about it.

Jordan didn't quit social media entirely, but he learned how to set boundaries—and that simple shift in self-discipline gave him back hours of his life.

How to Build Self-Discipline

1. **Start Small**: Don't try to overhaul your entire routine at once. Pick one habit—like waking up 10 minutes earlier or reading two pages of a book—and focus on that.
2. **Use Triggers**: Tie new habits to something you already do. For example, if you want to start journaling, do it right after brushing your teeth.
3. **Remove Temptations**: If your phone is distracted during homework, put it in another room.
4. **Reward Yourself**: Celebrate small wins. Treat yourself to something you enjoy after sticking to a habit for a week.

The Myth of Motivation

A common misconception is that you need to feel motivated to be disciplined. But motivation is fleeting—it comes and goes based on your mood. Self-discipline, on the other hand, is about showing up even when you don't feel like it.

Think about professional athletes, musicians, or writers. They don't wait for inspiration to strike before they practice—they've built routines that help them succeed.

The Story of Akshat's Second Chance

Akshat's goal was to write a research paper good enough to be entered into a national competition. But every time he sat down to write, he felt stuck. The pressure to write something perfect made him procrastinate. Weeks went by, and the deadline loomed closer.

Finally, Akshat promised himself: *"No more excuses."* He created a schedule: one hour of writing every morning, no matter what. The first few sessions were rough—his ideas felt clumsy, and he kept second-guessing himself. But he pushed through.

By the end of the month, Akshat had a draft. It wasn't perfect, but it was done. He revised, improved, and submitted it just before the deadline. Two months later, he received an email: his paper had been selected for publication.

Your Self-Discipline Challenge

This week, pick one small habit you want to build. It could be:

- ❖ *Reading for 10 minutes a day.*
- ❖ *Drinking water instead of soda.*
- ❖ *Practicing a skill for 15 minutes.*

Write it down, set a reminder, and commit to it for seven days. Track your progress and reflect on how it made you feel at the end of the week.

Why Self-Discipline Shapes Leaders

Self-discipline isn't about punishment—it's about empowerment. It's the key to becoming the person you've always wanted to be. When you show up for yourself—consistently, even in small ways—you build a life that reflects your values and dreams.

Just like Maya at the pool, Jordan during his social media detox, and Akshat at his desk, your moments of self-discipline will add up to something bigger than you ever imagined. When the temptation to quit shows up, remember you're not building habits for today—you're building your future.

Confidence – Believing in Your Potential

Confidence. It's one of those words people throw around a lot— *"Just be confident!"* They say, as if flipping a switch could make you feel invincible. But here's the truth: confidence doesn't magically appear overnight. It's not something you either have or don't have. It's something you build, bit by bit, through experience, practice, and resilience.

Confidence is like a muscle. The more you use it, the stronger it becomes. And just like muscles can feel sore after a tough challenge, your confidence might waver after setbacks. But the key is to keep showing up for yourself, even when things are hard.

The Story of Ekam: The Fear of the Spotlight

Ekam was smart, funny, and full of ideas—when he was with his close friends. But in public? It was like someone pressed mute. The thought of speaking up in class or presenting in front of an audience made his heart pound and his palms sweat.

One day, his English teacher assigned a project where each student had to deliver a speech about a personal story. Ekam felt like the world was closing in on him. Public speaking was his worst nightmare. He thought about calling in sick or asking for an extension. But deep down, he knew he couldn't avoid it forever.

So, Ekam planned. Instead of trying to memorize the entire speech in one go, he broke it down into small chunks. He practiced in front of a mirror, recording himself to hear how he sounded. Then, he took a more significant step—he practiced in front of his little sister, who clapped after every sentence, even when he stumbled. Ekam's hands still trembled the day of the presentation end as he walked to the front of the room, but this time, something was different. Instead of focusing on his nerves, he focused on the story he wanted to share. He locked eyes with a friend in the audience, who gave him an encouraging nod, and he took a deep breath.

Ekam didn't just get through his speech—he owned it. When he finished, the class erupted in applause. His teacher said, *"That was one of the most heartfelt speeches I've ever heard."* Ekam felt true confidence for the first time—not the absence of fear, but the courage to move forward despite it.

What Confidence Is (And What It Isn't)

Confidence isn't about being the loudest person in the room or pretending you have all the answers.

- ❖ ***Confidence is calm, not cocky.*** *It's knowing your worth without needing to prove it to everyone.*
- ❖ ***Confidence is earned, not inherited.*** *You build it by showing up, trying, and learning from setbacks.*
- ❖ ***Confidence is about progress, not perfection.*** *It's about taking pride in your efforts, not just the outcome.*

The Science of Confidence

Did you know that confidence can change how your brain works? Studies show that when you believe you can succeed, your brain releases dopamine—a chemical that boosts motivation and focus. This belief can improve your performance. In other words, confidence isn't just a "feel-good" emotion—it's a tool that can help you perform better.

But here's the catch: confidence doesn't come first. Action does. You don't wait to feel confident before taking a step forward—you take a step forward, and confidence follows.

The Story of Grace's Soccer Comeback

Grace had always been passionate about soccer, but her confidence took a nosedive after she missed a crucial penal. She started doubting herself every time she stepped onto the field.

Her coach pulled her aside one day and said, *"You're not defined by one moment. Every great player has missed a shot. The only difference is that they keep playing."*

Grace decided to permit herself to fail during practice. Instead of obsessing over being perfect, she focused on learning. Slowly, the fear that had clouded her mind lifted. In the next season's final game, Grace faced another penalty kick. This time, she didn't think about the last miss. She planted her feet, took a breath, and kicked. The ball soared into the net.

How to Build Unshakable Confidence

1. **Start with Small Wins**: Confidence grows from success, even small ones. Set manageable challenges for yourself and celebrate when you achieve them.
2. **Reframe Self-Talk**: Pay attention to how you talk to yourself. Instead of saying, *"I'm terrible at this,"* try saying, *"I'm learning and improving."*
3. **Take Up Space**: Walk with your head held high and shoulders back. Your body language will trick your brain into feeling more confident.
4. **Prepare, but Don't Overthink**: Preparation builds confidence, but overthinking can paralyze you. Know when to stop practicing and trust yourself.

5. **Embrace Failure as Feedback**: Remember failure is the opposite of success—it's part of it. Each mistake teaches you something valuable.

Why Comparison Kills Confidence

It's easy to scroll through social media and compare yourself to people who seem to have it all together. But here's what you don't see: their struggles, doubts, and behind-the-scenes moments. Comparing yourself to others is like comparing your practice footage to someone else's highlight reel—it's not a fair comparison.

Confidence comes from knowing that your journey is yours alone. Instead of measuring yourself against others, focus on how far you've come.

The Confidence Journal Challenge

Confidence isn't built in a day—it's built-in moments. This week, I start a "Confidence Journal." Every day, write down one thing you did well, no matter how small. Maybe you raised your hand in class, aced a quiz, or had a tough conversation. These moments add up.

For an extra challenge, write down one positive thing someone else said about you that stuck with you. When self-doubt creeps in, reflect on your journal and remind yourself of your strengths.

Why Confidence Makes You a Better Leader

Confidence isn't about being fearless—it's about being brave. When you're confident, you inspire others to believe in themselves, too. Leaders who radiate confidence create an atmosphere where people feel safe to take risks, share ideas, and grow.

Think back to Ekam's story. He didn't become confident overnight. He became confident by showing up, step by step until the fear that once controlled him became something he could face.

Your journey to confidence starts the same way—with a tiny, brave step forward.

CHAPTER 8

EMOTIONAL INTELLIGENCE

UNDERSTANDING YOURSELF

AND OTHERS

Emotional intelligence—two big words that sound like they belong in a psychology textbook rather than your daily life. But here's the truth: emotional intelligence (or EQ) is one of the most essential skills you'll ever learn. It's not just about understanding how you feel—navigating relationships, managing emotions, and handling challenges with empathy and self-awareness.

Think about your favorite leaders or role models. What makes them stand out? Is it just their talent or intelligence? Probably not. The leaders who inspire us often can stay calm under pressure, listen before they speak, and know how to uplift the people around them. That's emotional intelligence in action.

The Story of Rudransh: The Power of Listening

Rudransh was known as "the fixer." If his friends had a problem, they went to him. If there was drama in the group chat, Rudransh tried to calm things down. But while Rudransh was great at solving issues, there was one thing he wasn't so good at—*listening without fixing*.

One afternoon, his best friend, Alex, walked up to him after school, looking at my history presentation," Alex muttered. "The teacher called me out in front of the whole class."

Rudransh jumped in immediately. "Next time, you should practice more in front of a mirror. And maybe you can ask for extra credit work to make up for it."

Alex's shoulders slumped. "I don't need advice right now. I just need you to listen."

That hit Rudransh like a brick. He realized that sometimes people don't want solutions—they want to feel heard. Instead of responding with advice, Rudransh tried something different. He said, *"That sounds tough. I'm sorry you had to go through that."*

Alex's face softened. The tension in his voice eased as he opened up about how embarrassed he'd felt in class. Rudransh didn't have to "fix" anything; being there made all the difference.

Why Emotional Intelligence Matters

Emotional intelligence isn't about being perfect or pretending to have all the answers. It's about being present, being curious, and treating yourself and others with kindness. Here's why EQ is so powerful:

1. **Improves Relationships**: When you understand your emotions, you're better able to understand the feelings of others, which leads to stronger connections.

164

2.   **Reduces Conflict**: Empathy helps you see things from someone else's perspective, making it easier to resolve disagreements calmly.

3.   **Boosts Leadership Skills**: Great leaders aren't just intelligent but emotionally aware. They know how to inspire, motivate, and support their teams.

4.   **Builds Resilience**: EQ helps you navigate stress and setbacks without letting your emotions take over.

Understanding Your Own Emotions

Think of your emotions like the dashboard of a car. When the fuel light comes on, you don't ignore it—you pull over and fill up the tank. The same goes for your emotions. They're signals, not roadblocks. Your brain tells you something that needs attention if you're feeling stressed, anxious, or frustrated.

But here's the catch: emotions can be tricky. Sometimes, they appear like flashing neon signs; other times, they're subtle, like a soft hum in the background. Learning to recognize your feelings is the first step to managing them.

The Story of Emma's "Volcano Moments"

Emma was the kind of person who bottled things up. She'd stay quiet when someone hurt her feelings and pretend everything was fine. But inside, she was like a volcano—her frustration built and built until, one day, she'd erupt over something minor, like a missing charger or a sarcastic comment.

One day, after an argument with her sister over something trivial, Emma's mom asked her, *"What's going on?"* Emma burst into tears and admitted that she'd been overwhelmed with school, friend drama, and her responsibilities on the volleyball team.

Her mom handed her a journal and said, *"You don't have to wait until you explode. Try writing things down when you feel them."*

At first, Emma wasn't sure how it would help. But she gave it a shot. Each night, she wrote down her frustrations, fears, and victories—no matter how small. Over time, she noticed that naming her feelings made them more manageable. She wasn't suppressing her emotions anymore—she was understanding them.

How to Strengthen Your Emotional Intelligence

1. **Name Your Emotions**: Instead of saying, *"I'm fine,"* name your feelings. Are you disappointed when you're upset? Angry? Nervous? Naming your emotions helps you process them.

2. **Pause Before Reacting**: When you feel your emotions rising, pause for a few seconds before reacting. Deep breath can make the difference between responding calmly and snapping.

3. **Empathy Check**: When someone's upset, practice empathy by asking yourself, *"How would I feel in their shoes?"*

4. **Ask Questions, Don't Assume**: Instead of assuming why someone is upset, ask, *"How are you feeling?"* or *"What's on*

your mind?" Sometimes, understanding is just one question away.

Why Self-Compassion Matters

A big part of emotional intelligence is learning to be kind to yourself. You're not a robot—you will make mistakes, have bad days, and feel overwhelmed sometimes. That doesn't make you weak—it makes you human.

When things go wrong, practice self-compassion by talking to yourself like you'd talk to a friend. Instead of saying, *"I messed up. I'm such a failure,"* try saying, *"I made a mistake, but I'm learning from it."*

The Story of Rudransh's Leadership Moment

Months after his conversation with Alex, Rudransh was elected student council president. During one of their meetings, there was a heated debate about the upcoming school event. Voices grew louder, and the atmosphere felt tense.

Instead of trying to "win" the argument, Rudransh used his emotional intelligence. He held up his hand and said, *"Let's pause for a second. I want to make sure everyone feels heard."*

He went around the room, letting everyone know their concerns without interruption. The room slowly calmed down as people realized they weren't being ignored.

By the end of the meeting, they had a solid plan—and they'd grown closer as a team. Later, one of the council members told

Rudransh, *"You're one of the only leaders who makes people feel seen."* That, more than any title or achievement, made Rudransh proud.

Your Emotional Intelligence Challenge

This week, try one of these EQ-building exercises:

❖ *Mirror Check: When feeling a strong emotion, look in the mirror and name what you see—your body language, your facial expression, and ask yourself, "What is this emotion trying to tell me?"*

❖ *Empathy Practice: The next time a friend vents to you, listen immediately without offering advice, be present, and say, "I'm here for you."*

❖ *Gratitude Journal: Each night, write down one moment you handled your emotions gracefully or supported someone else emotionally.*

Why Emotional Intelligence Creates Better Leaders

Emotional intelligence doesn't just make you a better friend or teammate—it makes you a better leader. Leaders with high EQ create spaces where people feel safe, supported, and understood. They don't just lead with their heads but with their hearts, too.

Think about Rudransh's story. His ability to listen, empathize, and stay calm made him a leader people trusted. You have that same potential within you. With practice, you can build emotional intelligence that helps you navigate life's ups and downs with resilience and compassion.

Empathy – The Key to Building Meaningful Connections

Imagine walking down the hallway at school and noticing someone sitting alone at lunch with their head down, poking at their food. You think, *"Should I say something? Would it make a difference?"* These moments happen all the time. They seem small, but they're the building blocks of something powerful: empathy.

Empathy isn't just about feeling sorry for someone—it's about understanding their perspective and being present with their feelings. It's about stepping into someone else's world, even if just for a moment, and saying, *"I see you. I get it."*

In a world where so much communication happens through screens and emojis, genuine human connection can sometimes feel distant. But empathy is what brings people together. It turns acquaintances into friends, teammates into family, and classmates into allies.

The Story of Meena: The Quiet Connection

Meena wasn't the loudest person in the room. She didn't love big crowds or group projects and was known for sitting quietly at the edge of conversations. But while some people mistook her quietness for shyness, Meena had a strength that not everyone noticed: she was an incredible listener.

One afternoon, her friend Elena burst into the library, visibly upset. She dropped her backpack onto the table and muttered, *"Why is everything so hard?"*

Meena closed her book, leaned forward, and simply said, *"What happened?"*

Elena's eyes filled with tears as she explained that her parents were fighting at home, and she felt caught in the middle. Meena didn't interrupt. She didn't rush to give advice. She just listened— really listened. When Elena finished speaking, Meena said, *"That sounds hard. I'm so sorry you're going through that."*

Elena exhaled deeply as though a weight had been lifted. She later told Meena, *"You didn't try to fix it. You just let me feel heard. That's what I needed most."*

That day, Meena realized something: empathy doesn't require grand gestures or perfect words. Sometimes, the most powerful way to show empathy is simply to be there, fully present, without judgment.

What Empathy Is (And What It Isn't)

Let's break down what empathy means:

* ❖ ***Empathy is listening, not fixing.*** *It understands someone's feelings and does not rush to offer solutions.*
* ❖ ***Empathy is presence, not perfection.*** *It's showing up, even when you don't have the perfect thing to say.*
* ❖ ***Empathy is perspective, not assumption.*** *It's putting yourself in someone's shoes, even if you've never walked their path.*

Why Empathy Feels Hard Sometimes

It's not always easy to practice empathy. Sometimes, instead of saying the wrong thing or feeling uncomfortable with someone else's pain. Other times, we're distracted by our ss or struggles. But empathy isn't about having all the answers—it's about being willing to sit with someone in their experience.

The Story of Marcus and the Group Project

Marcus was assigned to work with Meena on a history project. Marcus was loud, opinionated, and convinced that his ideas were the best. Meena preferred to observe and take her time before speaking up. Their first meeting was awkward—Marcus dominated the conversation while Meena barely said anything.

But instead of shutting down, Meena approached the project with empathy. She asked Marcus, *"Why do you feel so strongly about this idea?"* At first, Marcus was defensive, but then he admitted, *"I just really want this to go well. I feel like I need to prove I'm good at something."*

Meena nodded and said, *"I get that. We should do our best, even if we have different styles."*

By the end of their project, something surprising happened: Marcus stopped interrupting as much, and Meena started contributing more confidently. Their empathy for each other's experiences made them a stronger team. They didn't just complete the project—they became friends.

Why Empathy Is a Superpower

Empathy isn't just a "nice-to-have" trait—it's a superpower that can change your life and the lives of those around you. Here's why:

1. **It Strengthens Relationships**: People are more likely to trust and open up to you. When they feel understood.
2. **It Reduces Conflict**: Empathy helps you see things from someone else's point of view, making disagreements less about winning and more about understanding.
3. **It Builds Leadership Skills**: Great leaders lead with empathy. They inspire others by making them feel valued and heard.
4. **It Cultivates Kindness**: Empathy encourages acts of kindness—sometimes small, sometimes life-changing.

How to Practice Empathy

1. **Listen Without Distractions**: When someone's talking to you, put down your phone and give them your full attention.
2. **Ask, Don't Assume**: Instead of assuming how someone feels, ask questions like, *"How are you feeling?"* or *"What can I do to help?"*
3. **Validate Their Emotions**: Let people know their feelings are valid. Even if you don't fully understand, saying, *"That sounds difficult,"* can mean the world.
4. **Be Patient**: Sometimes, people need time to open up. Let them know you're there when they're ready.

The Empathy Challenge

This week, choose one person in your life—maybe a friend, family member, or classmate—and practice empathy with them. When they talk, focus on listening without planning your response. Let them feel heard without rushing to solve their problem.

For an extra challenge, reach out to someone you don't usually talk to—a classmate who eats lunch alone or someone who seems quiet in your group—and show them kindness. A simple *"Hey, how's your day going?"* can make a more significant impact than you think.

Why Empathy Makes You a Stronger Leader

Empathy doesn't make you "soft"—it makes you strong. It takes courage to sit with someone's pain or to admit you don't have all the answers. Leaders with empathy create spaces where people feel safe, supported, and empowered to be authentic.

Meena didn't need to shout to be a leader. Her quiet strength came from her ability to make others feel seen. When you lead with empathy, you're not just making connections but building a community where people feel like they belong.

Building Bridges – How to Foster Mutual Respect and Trust

Respect and trust are like the twin pillars holding up any meaningful relationship—between friends, family members, teammates, or strangers. But here's the thing: respect and trust aren't automatic. They don't appear out of nowhere. They're built over time, brick by brick, through words, actions, and intentions.

Think about your favorite bridge—the Golden Gate, Brooklyn, or even a local one you cross daily. Bridges don't just connect two points—they bring people and places together. Building bridges between people works the same way. It takes effort, precision, and patience. And just like a bridge needs regular maintenance to stay strong, relationships need ongoing care to keep trust and respect intact.

The Story of Caleb and the Group Assignment Dilemma

Caleb was assigned a group project with three classmates for his U.S. History class. One of his teammates, Ava, was notoriously unreliable. She was intelligent but always late and often distracted. Caleb's first instinct was to take over the entire project himself. *"If I do it all, I know it'll get done right,"* he thought.

But something his mom had told him stuck in his mind: *"When you don't give people a chance, you rob them of the opportunity to grow."*

Instead of taking control, Caleb decided to build trust. He sat down with his group and said, *"Let's split this up so we all have a part we're excited about. I know things come up, but let's agree to check in twice weekly to stay on track."*

To Caleb's surprise, Ava delivered her part of the project early. She even added extra research that impressed their teacher.

Later, she thanked Caleb for giving her the space to contribute without judgment.

In that moment, Caleb realized that respect isn't just about how you treat people—it's about the space you create for others to show up as their best selves.

Why Respect and Trust Matter

When you build respect and trust in your relationships, you:

- ❖ *Strengthen Connections: People feel safe sharing their ideas, fears, and dreams with you.*
- ❖ *Encourage Collaboration: Teams with trust perform better because they work as a unit instead of competing against each other.*
- ❖ *Prevent Misunderstandings: When you approach others respectfully, conflicts are more likely to be resolved calmly.*

The Story of Layla's Cross-Cultural Exchange

Layla signed up for her school's international exchange program and was paired with a student named Hiroshi from Japan. She was excited but nervous. Would they have anything in common? What if they didn't understand each other's jokes or traditions?

On Hiroshi's first day at Layla's school, she noticed he was quiet and reserved during lunch. Layla could tell he was overwhelmed. Instead of forcing conversation, she asked, *"Hey, Hiroshi, do you want me to show you around?"* Hiroshi nodded, grateful for the kindness without pressure.

As the weeks went on, they learned from each other. Layla taught Hiroshi about her favorite American traditions—like pumpkin carving at Halloween—and Hiroshi taught Layla about Japanese calligraphy and his family's annual cherry blossom picnic.

By the end of the semester, they weren't just exchange partners—they were close friends. Layla realized trust wasn't built with big, dramatic moments—it grew in small acts of kindness, patience, and understanding.

The Foundations of Mutual Respect and Trust

Building bridges between people requires key elements:

1. **Consistency**: Trust is built when your actions match your words over time. Be reliable and follow through on commitments.
2. **Active Listening**: Respect isn't just about agreeing—it's about giving others the space to express themselves without feeling dismissed.
3. **Empathy**: Putting yourself in someone else's shoes helps you understand their perspective, even if it's different from yours.
4. **Vulnerability**: Sharing your own experiences and emotions can deepen trust. It shows others that you're human, too.

Why Trust Can Be Hard to Build (But Easy to Break)

Trust takes time to earn but only a moment to lose. It can be broken by dishonesty, betrayal, or even small actions that make people feel unseen or disrespected. But the good news is that broken trust can be repaired—if you're willing to put in the effort.

The Story of Meena and the Broken Promise

Meena and her best friend Jasmine had made plans to study together for their big math test. But the night before, Jasmine bailed to hang out with another group of friends. Meena was hurt—not because Jasmine canceled, but because she didn't even text to explain.

Instead of ignoring it, Meena decided to be honest. She said, *"Jasmine, I get things come up, but it hurt that you didn't tell me. I felt like I wasn't important."*

Jasmine looked down and said, *"I'm so sorry. I didn't think it would matter, but I now see it did."*

That conversation wasn't easy, but it rebuilt their friendship. Meena didn't hold a grudge, and Jasmine tried to be more thoughtful in the future. Their friendship became more substantial because they learned to communicate honestly and respectfully.

How to Build Bridges in Your Relationships

1. **Be Honest, But Kind**: When you give feedback, focus on the issue, not the person. Instead of saying, *"You're always*

late," try, *"I feel stressed when we don't start on time because I want us to finish early."*

2. **Apologize When You Mess Up**: A sincere apology can go a long way in repairing trust. Admit when you're wrong, and show you're committed to making things right.
3. **Respect Boundaries**: Everyone has their limits. Respecting someone's time, space, and feelings shows that you care.
4. **Celebrate Wins Together**: Whether it's a small achievement or a significant milestone, celebrate with the people who've supported you.

The "Bridge-Building" Challenge

This week, think about someone in your life who you've drifted apart from or disagreed with. Reach out to them—not to fix everything overnight, but to reopen the lines of communication. It could be as simple as, *"Hey, I've been thinking about you. How's everything going?"*

For an extra challenge, practice giving someone your full attention during a conversation—no phone, no distractions. Let them feel heard and valued.

Why Respect and Trust Make You a Stronger Leader

Respect and trust aren't just nice qualities—they're the foundation of outstanding leadership. Leaders who foster trust create teams where people feel safe to share their ideas and take risks. Leaders who show respect earn respect in return.

Think about Caleb, Layla, and Meena. Their ability to build bridges didn't just strengthen their relationships—it made them leaders who others could depend on. You have that same power within you. By choosing empathy, honesty, and consistency, you're not just building connections and a community where everyone feels valued.

Take the first step. Build the bridge. You might be surprised at how much stronger your relationships and confidence become.

CHAPTER 9

RESILIENCE – BOUNCING

BACK FROM SETBACKS

Resilience. It's a word that gets thrown around a lot—like it's some kind of secret superpower that only lucky few have. But resilience isn't about being unbreakable or fearless. It's not about never falling. It's about how you get back up after you've hit the ground.

Life can feel like a rollercoaster, especially as a teenager. One day, you're on top of the world after taking a test or winning a game. The next, you're spiraling because something didn't go as planned. But what separates those who thrive from those who get stuck isn't the absence of failure—it's how they respond to it.

Resilience is the ability to face setbacks, disappointments, and failures and keep moving forward.

The Story of Varun: The Road to Recovery

Varun was a star track athlete at his high school. His speed was unmatched, and everyone expected him to break the state record in the upcoming season. But during a routine practice, something happened that changed everything.

Varun felt a sharp pain in his leg as he rounded the last bend of the track. He stumbled, fell to the ground, and couldn't stand up. The diagnosis: a torn ligament. He was benched for months.

At first, Varun was devastated. Running wasn't just something he did—it was a part of who he was. Without it, he felt lost. He scrolled through social media, watching his teammates post pictures of practices and meets he couldn't attend. The fear of being forgotten or replaced gnawed at him.

But one evening, as he sat on his porch staring at his crutches, his mom handed him a journal. *"Write it down,"* she said. *"All the frustration, the fear, the anger. Get it out of your head."*

At first, Varun rolled his eyes. How was writing supposed to fix anything? But later that night, when sleep wouldn't come, he opened the journal and scribbled down his thoughts. Slowly, something shifted. Writing became a way for him to process the pain instead of drowning in it.

Varun realized that while he couldn't control his injury, he could control how he responded. He focused on his physical therapy like it was a championship. He showed up to every practice—not as a runner, but as a teammate—offering encouragement and support from the sidelines.

Months later, when Varun was finally cleared to run again, something incredible happened. His first race back wasn't his fastest, but it was his proudest. He had bounced back—not just as an athlete, but as someone who knew his worth didn't depend on trophies or records.

Why Resilience Matters

Resilience isn't just about bouncing back after significant life events—it's about how you handle the everyday challenges, too. Whether it's failing a quiz, not making the team, or feeling left out by friends, resilience helps you:

1. **Stay Grounded**: Instead of spiraling into negative thoughts, you learn to stay calm and refocus.
2. **Adapt to Change**: Life rarely goes according to plan. Resilience helps you adjust and keep moving forward.
3. **Build Confidence**: The more challenges you overcome, the more you believe in your ability to handle future obstacles.

The Science of Resilience

Your brain is wired to protect you from pain—emotional or physical. When you experience a setback, your brain sends out stress signals that trigger feelings of fear, disappointment, or self-doubt. But here's the good news: resilience is like a muscle. The more you exercise it, the stronger it gets.

Studies show that people who practice resilience-building habits—like positive self-talk, problem-solving, and mindfulness— experience less stress and recover more quickly from setbacks.

The Story of Bella's Lost Election

Bella had dreamed of being student body president since the first year. She poured her heart into her campaign—late nights making posters, practicing her speech, and meeting with classmates to share her ideas. On election day, she stood on stage, hopeful and excited.

When the results were announced, Bella's heart sank. She lost by 12 votes. She smiled through the announcement, but inside, she felt crushed.

That night, Bella's dad said something stuck with her: *"You didn't lose. You learned."* At first, she didn't want to hear it. But after some reflection, she realized that running for president had taught her so much—how to speak in front of a crowd, handle pressure, and connect with people.

The following year, Bella ran for vice president instead of president. She used everything she'd learned and ran an even more vigorous campaign. She won in a landslide.

How to Strengthen Your Resilience

1. **Reframe Failure**: Instead of seeing failure as the end, see it as feedback. Ask yourself, *"What did I learn from this?"*
2. **Practice Self-Compassion**: Treat yourself like you'd treat a friend going through a tough time. Remind yourself that setbacks don't define you.
3. **Focus on What You Can Control**: When things go wrong, shift your energy toward the things you *can* influence.
4. **Build a Support System**: Surround yourself with people who lift you, and list and remind yourself of your strengths.

The "Resilience Reset" Exercise

The next time you face a setback, try this three-step exercise:

1. **Pause and Breathe**: Take a few deep breaths to calm your body and clear your mind.
2. **Reflect**: Write down what happened, how you felt, and what you can learn from the experience.
3. **Plan Your Next Step**: Identify one small action you can take to move forward asking for help, adjusting your approach, or simply taking a break to reset.

Why Resilience Builds Strong Leaders

Resilient leaders don't avoid challenges—they embrace them. They know that failure isn't a dead end—it's a steppingstone. When you practice resilience, you:

❖ *Show others that it's okay to struggle and bounce back.*
❖ *Build the kind of inner strength that inspires others.*
❖ *Create a mindset where setbacks are seen as temporary, not permanent.*

Think about Varun. His injury could have defined him, but instead, it became a chapter in his story—not the whole book. The next time life knocks you down, remember you have everything you need to rise again.

CHAPTER 10

VISION – SEEING THE BIG PICTURE AND SETTING GOALS FOR THE FUTURE

Close your eyes for a moment and picture your future. What do you see? Maybe you're standing on a stage, delivering a speech that moves people. Maybe you're in a lab, working on a discovery that changes the world. Or maybe you're surrounded by people whose lives you've made better in some way. Whatever your vision is, it starts here—not someday in the distant future, but now.

Having a vision doesn't mean having all the answers. It means knowing where you want to go, even if you don't yet know every twist and turn along the way. Your vision is your internal compass—it keeps you moving in the right direction, even when the path gets hard or when things don't go as planned.

The Story of Vinay: The Unexpected Detour

Vinay had always dreamed of becoming a journalist. He imagined traveling the world, interviewing fascinating people, and sharing stories that mattered. He had his sights set on a summer internship at a top newspaper—a steppingstone to his dream career.

He'd prepared for the interview for weeks, researching the company, practicing answers, and even ironing his best blazer.

But when the email arrived, it wasn't the news he'd hoped for. "Thank you for your application. Unfortunately, we've selected another candidate."

For days, Vinay felt crushed. He began doubting himself, wondering if his dream was slipping out of reach. But after a long talk with his older sister Bulbul, who had faced her own share of setbacks as a law student, he realized something important. "Your dream didn't disappear," Bulbul told him. "It just took a different path. The vision is still yours—you just need to find another way to get there."

Inspired by her words, Vinay found another opportunity—a smaller local magazine looking for student contributors. He poured his heart into every article he wrote, covering community stories that often went unnoticed. His work caught the attention of a journalist at the bigger paper—the very one he'd dreamed of working for. A few months later, that journalist offered him a mentorship, opening doors Vinay hadn't even imagined.

Vinay's vision didn't change—it expanded. He learned that setbacks weren't signs to give up; they were just redirections.

What Vision Really Means

Vision isn't about knowing every step of your journey—it's about having a sense of purpose that guides you, even when the details are unclear. Here's what vision looks like in real life:

A Clear "**Why**": Your vision starts with understanding why something matters to you. Why do you want to make an impact? Why does this dream excite you?

A Flexible "**How**": Your vision isn't a strict blueprint—it's a guiding star. Your approach may change, but your end goal remains.

A **Big Picture View**: Vision means zooming out and reminding yourself of your long-term goals, especially when short-term challenges pop up.

The Story of Bulbul's Pivot

Bulbul had always been passionate about making a difference in her community. She dreamed of working at a nonprofit that focused on justice and equality. She applied to every major organization she could find but kept getting rejection emails. Each one felt like a punch to the gut.

Instead of giving up, Bulbul decided to pivot. She asked herself, "What's one small step I can take toward my goal today?" She began volunteering with a local legal aid group, offering her time and skills where she could.

Her vision never changed—only the path she took. Months later, her volunteer work led to a full-time role at a nonprofit. The rejections that once felt like closed doors became steppingstones to something even more meaningful.

Why Vision Matters

It Keeps You Grounded: When you have a clear vision, you're less likely to be swayed by distractions or short-term setbacks.

It Fuels Motivation: Your vision reminds you why you started, especially when things get tough.

It Inspires Others: When people see someone pursuing a dream with clarity and purpose, it's contagious and motivates them to pursue their dreams.

How to Cultivate Your Vision

Visualize Your Future: Spend five minutes daily picturing what success looks and feels like. Be specific—where are you, who's with you, what are you doing?

Write a "Mission Statement" for Yourself: Describe your purpose and long-term goals in a few sentences. Keep it somewhere visible as a reminder.

Break It Down: Big visions can feel overwhelming. Break your goals into smaller, manageable steps you can work on every week.

Stay Open to Change: Your vision may stay the same, but the path might change—and that's okay.

The Vision Journal Challenge

This week, I start a Vision Journal. Write down your long-term goals and why they matter to you. Then, list three small actions you can take this month to move closer to that vision.

For an extra challenge, reflect on how your vision has evolved. What lessons have shaped it? What setbacks have made you stronger?

The Power of Sharing Your Vision

When you share your vision with others, something magical becomes more real. It's no longer just a thought in your mind; it's a goal you're working toward. Sharing your vision also invites others to support, collaborate, and hold you accountable.

Think about Vinay. When he shared his journalism dream with Bulbul, her encouragement helped him see past his setbacks. His vision grew more potent because he wasn't carrying it alone.

Why Vision Creates Leaders

Great leaders aren't just focused on the present—a vision for the future guides them. They inspire others to believe in what's possible, even when the path is unclear.

Your vision is your blueprint for the life you want to build. It doesn't have to be perfect, and it doesn't have to impress anyone else. It just has to matter to you.

So, what's your vision? What dream keeps you up at night, excited for what's ahead? Whatever it is, remember: every step you take today is a brick in the foundation of your future. You don't have to know every twist and turn—just take the next step with courage.

CHAPTER 11

LEADERSHIP IN THE AGE OF

AI AND BEYOND

The Changing Landscape of Careers and Leadership

Imagine waking up 20 years from now. The world has changed in ways we can't fully imagine today. Cars drive themselves, virtual reality is part of everyday life, and your friends are working jobs that didn't even exist when you were in high school. The pace of change is accelerating—and that change is being driven by technology, artificial intelligence (AI), and automation.

Now, think about this: some jobs people dreamed of 50 years ago have disappeared. In contrast, new jobs—like social media managers and app developers—didn't exist until recently. So, what does this mean for you as a future leader? It means you're stepping into a world where success will depend on your ability to **adapt, learn,** and **lead with resilience.**

The Shift from Routine to Innovation

In the past, most jobs required people to follow clear, predictable routines—show up, do the same tasks, and clock out. But today, automation and AI are taking over repetitive, routine jobs. What's left for humans? These are jobs that require creativity, emotional intelligence, and problem-solving.

Example: Think about how companies like Tesla use AI-powered robots to assemble cars. The robots handle the repetitive tasks, but humans must design new features, troubleshoot issues, and make decisions when something unexpected happens.

The same shift is happening in almost every industry—from healthcare to education, business to space exploration. Future leaders like you need to see the big picture and use creativity, empathy, and decision-making skills to navigate uncharted waters.

Story Spotlight: Savar's Innovation Challenge

Savar, a student council president at his high school, was tasked with creating a fundraising event for the school's robotics team. Instead of hosting the usual bake sale or car wash, he wanted to try something different—an online "hackathon for good," where teams could compete to solve real-world problems using AI tools and coding.

However, when he proposed the idea, some teachers were skeptical. "What if the tech breaks?" "Will people even understand how to participate?" they asked.

Savar didn't give up. He gathered a team of student volunteers and contacted local tech companies for support. He explained his vision: to raise money and inspire his classmates to learn about technology and innovation. His resilience paid off—the hackathon was a massive success, raising double the expected funds and sparking interest in tech careers among students who'd never coded before

Why This Matters to You

The world isn't slowing down. New challenges and opportunities will continue to emerge. As you prepare for your future, ask yourself:

1. How can I adapt when things don't go as planned?
2. How can I use technology as a tool, not a crutch?
3. How can I lead in ways that foster creativity and collaboration, even when AI is part of the process?

These are the questions that future leaders must answer. And the best part? You don't need to wait until you graduate or get your first job to start thinking like a leader. You can start by looking for ways to solve problems creatively, using digital tools to bring ideas to life, and collaborating with others to make an impact.

The Human Edge – Qualities AI Can't Replace

Imagine sitting across from the most innovative AI in the world. It can predict stock market trends, generate essays in seconds, and even help diagnose illnesses. But there's one thing it can't do—it can't feel. It can't understand what it means to comfort a struggling friend, the spark of excitement when two people collaborate on a bold new idea, or the courage it takes to make a tough decision when the stakes are high.

That's where you come in. The "human edge" consists of the qualities that no machine can replicate—qualities that make you indispensable as a leader.

1. Creativity and Imagination

AI can analyze patterns, but it can't dream. Your creativity allows you to make connections between ideas that seem unrelated and to envision solutions that haven't been thought of before.

Example: In her history class, Madison's group was assigned to create a presentation on ancient civilizations. While most groups created slideshows, Madison thought differently. "What if we make it interactive?" she suggested. Her team ended up designing a virtual museum that allowed their classmates to walk through ancient Rome using VR headsets. They didn't just ace the project—they set a new standard for creativity in their school.

Why It Matters: In a world where AI can generate content, your imagination sets you apart. Leaders like Madison don't just follow instructions—they reimagine possibilities and inspire others to think differently.

Challenge: The next time you're brainstorming ideas, challenge yourself to come up with three wild solutions. Sometimes, the craziest ideas spark the biggest breakthroughs.

2. Empathy and Emotional Intelligence

AI can detect patterns in tone and word choice, but it can't truly understand how someone feels. It doesn't know what it's like to feel nervous before a speech or heartbroken after a loss. Empathy is what allows you to connect with others and build trust.

Example: Josh, the captain of the school's basketball team, noticed that one of his teammates, Ethan, wasn't performing well during practice. Instead of yelling or getting frustrated, Josh pulled Ethan aside and asked, "Everything okay?" Ethan opened up about struggling with schoolwork and feeling overwhelmed. Josh didn't just listen—he helped Ethan decide to get tutoring and offered to shoot hoops with him after practice to build his confidence.

Why It Matters: Teams led by empathetic leaders perform better because they feel supported, not judged. Josh's empathy didn't just make him a better captain—it made his team stronger.

Challenge: The next time you notice someone struggling, ask, "What's going on?" and be present without trying to "fix" them. Sometimes, just listening makes a world of difference.

3. Ethical Decision-Making

AI makes decisions based on algorithms, not values. But as a leader, you have a moral compass that helps you make choices that are fair and just—even when those decisions aren't easy.

Example: Rachel, the editor of her school's newspaper, was asked to write an article about an unfair rule change affecting extracurricular clubs. The administration wanted the article to stay neutral, but Rachel believed it was important to highlight student concerns respectfully. Instead of writing a one-sided piece, she interviewed both the principal and student leaders to present a balanced, thoughtful story. The result? The article sparked a school-wide discussion that led to changes in the policy.

Why It Matters: Great leaders make decisions based on what's right, not just what's popular or easy. Rachel's courage to tell the truth in a fair way set her apart.

Challenge: When you're faced with a difficult decision, ask yourself, "What's the right thing to do—not just the easiest?"

4. Adaptability and Intuition

AI relies on data and past trends, but it struggles when things change unexpectedly. Your intuition—shaped by experience—helps you make decisions when the path forward isn't clear.

Example: During her school's annual talent show, Olivia was in charge of running the sound system. Ten minutes before the show began, the speakers stopped working. The crowd was growing restless, and the pressure was on. Instead of panicking, Olivia trusted her instincts. She quickly set up a backup Bluetooth speaker and asked the first performer to adjust their set to something acoustic. The show went on, and afterward, her teacher told her, "You saved the night."

Why It Matters: Leaders who stay calm and adaptable when things don't go according to plan are the ones who inspire trust. Olivia's quick thinking and calm response kept the event running smoothly and showed her team how to handle setbacks with grace.

Challenge: The next time something goes wrong, take a deep breath and ask yourself, "What's my next best move?" Adaptability isn't about having all the answers—it's about making the most of what you have in the moment.

The Leadership Mindset: Be Human, Stay Human

The qualities that make you human—creativity, empathy, ethics, and adaptability—are also the qualities that make you a great leader. And here's the thing: using technology doesn't mean losing your humanity. In fact, the most impactful leaders of tomorrow will be the ones who combine technology with humanity.

Think of it this way: AI might be the engine, but you're the driver. Without your vision, purpose, and intuition, even the most advanced machine can't move in the right direction.

Challenge: The "Human Edge" Journal

This week, keep a journal of moments when you use your "human edge." Did you show empathy to a friend? Did you come up with a creative solution during a group project? Did you make an ethical decision even when it wasn't an easy choice?

By reflecting on these moments, you'll see just how powerful your human qualities are—and how they'll shape your leadership journey.

Preparing for the Jobs of the Future

Close your eyes for a moment and think about the future. What kind of world do you see? Autonomous vehicles glide down streets, virtual assistants help with daily routines, and careers you've never heard of today—like "space mining analyst" or "AI ethics consultant"—are as normal as software developers are now.

Here's the reality: the jobs of tomorrow will be different from the jobs of today. Some careers will evolve, others will disappear, and entirely new industries will emerge. So, how can you, as a teenager, prepare for a world where change is the only constant? The key isn't to predict the future—it's to develop skills that make you ready for **any** future.

Adaptability Over Specificity

There's a famous saying in the business world: "Adapt or get left behind." This is truer today than ever before. Preparing for future jobs doesn't mean locking yourself into one field or mastering a single skill—it means learning how to be flexible, curious, and resourceful.

Ethan had always wanted to become a software engineer. He enrolled in coding classes, stayed late after school to practice, and even created his own app. But halfway through his junior year, he realized he was more excited about designing the look and feel of his apps than writing the code. Instead of feeling stuck, Ethan pivoted toward UX/UI (user experience/user interface) design—a field that combined his love for creativity and technology.

Ethan didn't abandon his coding knowledge—it gave him a unique edge as a designer. His ability to adapt not only helped him find a better fit but also made him more competitive when applying for internships.

The Three "Future-Ready" Skills

Lifelong Learning: The most successful future leaders are those who never stop learning. Whether it's reading articles about new trends, taking online courses, or asking questions, a mindset of continuous growth will set you apart.

Critical Thinking: Machines can process information, but they can't think critically or evaluate information for biases. Learn to ask questions like, "What's the bigger picture?" and "What are the potential consequences?"

Collaboration Across Disciplines: The jobs of tomorrow won't exist in silos. Future leaders will need to work across fields— like combining biology with tech in biotech companies or blending art and AI to create new forms of media.

The Importance of Being a "T-Shape" Learner

In the future, companies and organizations will seek what's called "T-shaped" individuals.

The vertical line of the "T" represents deep expertise in one field (e.g., data science, finance, or design).

The horizontal line of the "T" represents broad knowledge across multiple areas, like communication, leadership, and creativity.

Why It Matters: The combination of depth and breadth makes you adaptable. You might be an expert coder, but if you also understand how to lead a team, communicate your ideas, and think creatively, you'll be much more valuable.

Olivia was part of her school's environmental club, where she spearheaded a project to reduce cafeteria waste. Her club needed someone who could crunch the numbers on food waste (data analysis), someone to design posters for awareness (graphic design), and someone to negotiate with school administrators (communication and leadership).

Instead of assigning these roles to three different people, Olivia became a "T-shaped" leader. She learned enough about each role to guide her team and contribute where needed. Her ability to blend multiple skill sets made her a standout leader, and their campaign reduced waste by 40% in one semester.

Future Careers You Haven't Heard of Yet

The future job market will be filled with careers that seem strange or futuristic today. Here's a glimpse at what might be ahead:

AI Psychologist: Someone who works on training AI to understand human emotions better.

Space Architect: Someone who designs homes and habitats for living on Mars or the moon.

Virtual Experience Curator: Someone who creates immersive digital experiences for entertainment, education, and travel.

The possibilities are endless—and they all need one thing: leaders who can combine innovation with human-centered thinking.

How You Can Prepare Today

Follow Curiosity: What makes you excited to learn more? Whether it's robotics, creative writing, or environmental science, dive in. Your interests today can shape tomorrow's opportunities.

Practice "Learning to Learn": Instead of memorizing answers, focus on learning how to ask better questions and find information on your own.

Join Multidisciplinary Groups: Clubs, teams, and projects that mix different interests—like debate teams working with coding clubs or science fairs with art exhibits—help you develop the collaboration skills you'll need in the future.

Challenge: The "Future You" Blueprint

Imagine it's 10 years from now, and you're stepping into your dream job. What does your life look like? Write down:

1. The skills you'd need to excel in that role.
2. The steps you can take today to build those skills.
3. One new subject or hobby you can explore this month will broaden your horizons.

Why Future-Ready Leaders Are Game-Changers

The future isn't something that happens to you—it's something you help create. The leaders of tomorrow won't be the ones who know everything—they'll be the ones who are ready to learn, adapt, and collaborate across fields to solve problems we can't even predict yet.

The good news? You're already starting that journey. Every time you ask questions, try new things, and reflect on what you've learned, you're building the skills that will make you an unstoppable leader in a world full of change.

Leading with Vision in an Unknown Future

Imagine standing at the edge of a forest with no clear path ahead. You know where you want to go, but the way forward is uncharted and filled with unknowns. That's what the future looks like—not just for you, but for everyone stepping into leadership roles in a rapidly changing world.

When the future is uncertain, the leaders who thrive aren't the ones who have all the answers—they're the ones who can stay calm, stay focused, and keep their vision clear, even when the path isn't.

What It Means to Lead with Vision

Leading with vision means having a clear sense of purpose that guides your decisions, even when things get complicated. It's not about predicting every twist and turn—it's about staying anchored to what matters most.

201

Example: During the early days of space exploration, engineers at NASA faced countless unknowns. There was no manual for how to land a spacecraft on the moon or how to bring astronauts back safely. But their vision—landing on the moon— kept them focused, even when setbacks happened. Without that vision, the Apollo program might have given up after its first failure.

In your own life, having a vision is like creating a North Star—it doesn't remove the challenges, but it reminds you why you're moving forward in the first place.

The Power of "Why"

When things get tough, your "why" becomes your fuel. Why are you pursuing this goal? Why does it matter to you? Whether it's improving your grades, winning a debate, or starting a community project, your "why" will remind you that the work is worth it—even when you feel lost or discouraged.

Example: Marcus had a passion for music and wanted to launch a student music festival. But organizing the event was harder than he expected. The school's budget was tight, and there were constant scheduling conflicts. At one point, Marcus almost quit. But when he sat down with his best friend, she asked, *"Why did you want to do this in the first place?"* His answer was simple: *"Because I believe students deserve a space to express themselves."* That reminder reignited his drive, and Marcus found creative solutions—like partnering with local businesses to sponsor the event. The festival ended up being one of the school's most memorable events that year.

Staying Calm in the Face of Chaos

The future can feel chaotic, especially when things don't go as planned. But the best leaders know how to stay calm and keep their vision intact, even when the world feels upside down. This doesn't mean ignoring your feelings—it means learning to center yourself and focus on what you *can* control.

Challenge: When you're feeling overwhelmed, try the "3-Step Reset":

1. **Pause and breathe**: Take a few slow, deep breaths to clear your mind.
2. **Refocus**: Remind yourself of your long-term goal and why it matters.
3. **Take one small step**: Identify a single action you can take to move forward, no matter how small.

Leading with Vision in Uncertain Times

1. **Be Willing to Adjust the Plan**: Having a vision doesn't mean sticking rigidly to one plan. Sometimes, the "how" will change, but the "why" stays the same. Leaders who are adaptable but focused on their purpose can navigate unexpected challenges.
2. **Communicate Your Vision Clearly**: Whether you're leading a group project or rallying your team for a fundraiser, your vision becomes powerful when others understand and believe in it. Practice explaining your vision in simple, inspiring terms.

3. **Inspire Hope, Not Fear**: In times of uncertainty, people look to leaders for reassurance. Your belief in the future can inspire confidence in others.

Example: When a high school's student government faced the possibility of canceling prom due to budget cuts, their class president, Natalie, didn't panic. Instead, she rallied her team, outlined a new plan, and reminded everyone of their vision: *"This isn't just about a dance—it's about giving our class something to celebrate."* Her calm leadership not only saved prom, but it strengthened their class's sense of unity.

Vision vs. Short-Term Goals

It's easy to confuse a "to-do list" with a vision. Your vision is the big-picture goal that keeps you grounded, while your short-term goals are the steps that get you there.

Imagine building a puzzle. The picture on the box is your vision—it shows what you're working toward. The individual pieces you place are your short-term goals. Some pieces will fit right away, and others will take time. But every piece you place gets you closer to the full picture.

Challenge: Create Your Vision Board

A vision board is a visual reminder of your goals and dreams. Gather pictures, quotes, and words that represent what you want to achieve. It doesn't have to be perfect—what matters is that it inspires you. Place it somewhere you'll see it every day.

The Leaders of Tomorrow Start Today

No one can predict exactly what the future will look like, but one thing is certain: leaders who have a clear vision, who stay resilient through challenges, and who inspire others with their purpose will always have a place in shaping the future.

You don't have to have every step figured out today. But if you stay connected to your "why" and take small steps toward your vision, you'll be amazed at what you can accomplish.

Ethics and Responsibility in a Tech-Driven World

Imagine this: A social media platform develops an AI algorithm that can predict what users want to see before they even know it themselves. It increases engagement, but soon people realize they're being shown only one kind of information—reinforcing their opinions and silencing opposing views. This isn't science fiction—it's the reality of living in a world driven by technology.

As AI and tech grow more powerful, the need for ethical leadership grows with it. Leaders of tomorrow must not only understand how to use technology but also know how to use it responsibly, ensuring that innovation benefits everyone, not just a select few.

The Big Questions of Ethics

As a future leader, you'll face ethical questions that don't have simple answers:

❖ *Should AI decide who gets access to resources like scholarships or financial aid?*

❖ *Should companies collect personal data if it improves services but invades privacy?*

❖ *How do you balance progress with fairness?*

These questions will shape the world you live in, and the way you lead through them will define your legacy.

Story: Emma's Dilemma in the Debate Club

Emma was the president of her school's debate team, and one of their upcoming topics was "Should AI systems be allowed to grade student essays?" Emma knew this wasn't just a hypothetical debate—it was a real-world issue. Some schools were already using AI grading systems to save time. But Emma felt uneasy. Could a machine truly understand creativity or nuance the way a human could?

During the debate, Emma didn't just focus on technical pros and cons—she asked her team to discuss the ethical implications. What if students from different cultural backgrounds wrote in ways the AI wasn't trained to understand? What if it penalized creativity in favor of standardized answers? Her approach helped the team see beyond the surface and dig deeper into the ethical gray areas.

By the end of the debate, even the most tech-savvy team members agreed: innovation needs to be paired with responsibility.

Core Principles of Ethical Leadership in Tech

1. **Transparency:** Great leaders make sure people understand how and why decisions are made. Whether you're designing an AI app or leading a project, transparency builds trust.

2. **Accountability:** When mistakes happen—and they will—leaders take responsibility and learn from them. Avoiding blame and focusing on solutions shows integrity.

3. **Inclusivity:** Ethical leaders ensure that new technologies serve everyone, not just a privileged few. They ask questions like, *"Who might be left out?"* and *"Whose voice is missing?"*

Why Responsibility Matters

Technology can solve problems, but it can also create new ones. History has shown that breakthroughs like the internet and social media transformed the world—but they also brought challenges, like misinformation and privacy concerns. Future leaders like you have the power to shape how new tools are used.

Example: When developing a new app, ethical leaders don't just ask, *"Will this work?"* They ask, *"Is this the right thing to do?"*

Story: Jason's Innovation Fair Project

Jason was working on a facial recognition app for his school's Innovation Fair. The app was designed to make attendance tracking faster. But as he tested it, Jason noticed that it didn't always recognize the faces of students with darker skin tones. Instead of brushing it off, Jason researched why. He discovered that many facial recognition programs are trained using biased data.

Rather than presenting the app as-is, Jason turned his project into a case study on bias in AI. He proposed a plan for more inclusive data collection and earned the "Best Social Impact Award" for his work. Jason's leadership showed that innovation isn't just about solving problems—it's about making sure the solutions work for everyone.

Building Your Ethical Compass

1. **Ask "Who Benefits?"**: When using technology, consider who gains from it—and who might be left behind.
2. **Consider Long-Term Impact**: Think about how a decision will affect not just today, but the future.
3. **Speak Up**: If something feels wrong, don't stay silent. Ethical leaders have the courage to challenge the status quo.

Challenge: The "Ethics in Action" Journal

For one week, pay attention to ethical dilemmas in your daily life—whether it's a news story about privacy issues or a class discussion about fairness. Write down the situation and your thoughts:

❖ *What would you do as a leader in that situation?*
❖ *What questions would you ask to understand the issue better?*

Reflecting on these moments will sharpen your ability to lead with integrity and make thoughtful, ethical choices.

The Future Needs Responsible Leaders

The leaders of tomorrow will face challenges that don't exist today. But the skills to navigate them—integrity, empathy, and responsibility—will always be relevant. By asking the hard questions and standing up for what's right, you can be the kind of leader who not only embraces innovation but also ensures it's used to create a fairer, better world for everyone.

The Human Element in a Technological World

In a world driven by screens, algorithms, and data, it's easy to forget what makes us truly human. The world of tomorrow will be filled with virtual assistants, smart homes, and AI companions, but no machine can replace the power of human connection, kindness, and intuition.

Why Human Connection Matters

Imagine two people applying for the same leadership role—one is brilliant at analyzing data, and the other knows how to make every member of their team feel valued and motivated. Who would you want to follow?

Data-driven decisions matter, but leaders who understand the **emotions, strengths, and challenges** of their team members build stronger, more resilient organizations.

Example: When a robotics team at a high school faced multiple failures during competitions, their captain, Logan, didn't just focus on fixing technical issues. He spent time listening to his teammates, understanding their frustrations, and reminding them why they started. The team didn't just improve their robotics skills—they grew closer, worked better together, and won the next regional competition.

Balancing Technology with Humanity

1. **Empathy Over Efficiency**: Being fast and efficient is great, but empathy creates trust and loyalty.
2. **Collaboration Over Automation**: Use technology to support teamwork, not to replace it.
3. **Presence Over Multitasking**: No app or device can replace the power of being fully present during important moments—whether in a conversation or a team project.

Challenge: Practice Active Listening

The next time you're in a conversation, put away your phone and give the other person your full attention. Notice how much more meaningful the connection feels when you're focused, not distracted.

The Takeaway

As technology becomes more advanced, leaders who prioritize human values will stand out. By staying grounded in empathy, respect, and genuine connection, you can lead in ways that machines never will.

A Call to Action

The future is unwritten, and you hold the pen. Every choice you make, every skill you develop, and every challenge you face is shaping the kind of leader you're becoming. As you've seen throughout this chapter, the world of tomorrow will need leaders who are adaptable, compassionate, and unafraid to ask tough questions.

Leadership Starts Today

You don't have to wait for a big title or a formal role to be a leader. Leadership begins with small moments—helping a classmate who's struggling, speaking up for what's right, or taking initiative in a group project. These moments build the habits that will prepare you to take on bigger responsibilities in the future.

What the World Needs from You

1. **Curiosity**: Be open to learning new things, even when they seem outside your comfort zone.
2. **Courage**: Don't be afraid to lead, even when you're unsure of the outcome.
3. **Compassion**: Remember that leadership isn't about being the smartest in the room—it's about lifting others up and creating an environment where everyone can succeed.

Story: Ellie's Community Project

Ellie, a high school sophomore, noticed that some of the younger students in her neighborhood didn't have access to after-school programs. Instead of waiting for someone else to step in, she started organizing free weekly workshops in her garage—everything from homework help to creative writing.

At first, only three kids showed up. But Ellie didn't quit. She reached out to local businesses for support, and soon, she had enough resources to host sessions at a local community center. Two years later, the program grew into a nonprofit that provided mentorship to dozens of students. Ellie didn't have all the answers when she started—but she led with heart and persistence.

Your Leadership Journey

Just like Ellie, you don't have to have everything figured out to make a difference. What matters most is that you begin. The world is evolving, and the future is filled with challenges—and opportunities—that only bold, thoughtful leaders can tackle.

So, here's the call to action:

- **Take the first step**: Whether it's joining a club, starting a project, or speaking up in class, choose one way to practice leadership today.
- **Keep learning**: The best leaders never stop learning—about themselves, their community, and the world.
- **Inspire others**: Leadership isn't a solo journey. Lift others as you rise.

Final Thought

As you step forward, remember that the future doesn't just happen—it's built by people like you. By staying true to your values and leading with purpose, you have the power to shape a world that's better, kinder, and more inspiring than ever before.

The question isn't, *"Will you be a leader someday?"* The real question is, *"What kind of leader will you be?"*

CHAPTER 12

KEY TAKEAWAYS AND NEXT STEPS

As you reach the final chapter of this book, take a moment to reflect on the incredible journey you've been on. You've learned how to find your voice, lead with empathy, solve problems creatively, and prepare for a future shaped by technology. But leadership isn't just about what you've learned—it's about what you do next.

This chapter is designed to help you review key lessons and create an action plan for continuous growth. Leadership isn't a finish line—it's a lifelong practice.

Summary of Leadership Lessons

Let's revisit the most important skills you've gained:

❖ *Self-Awareness and Vision: Great leaders know their strengths, their values, and their long-term goals.*
❖ *Communication and Public Speaking: Your words can inspire action when you speak with confidence and clarity.*
❖ *Debate and Critical Thinking: The ability to craft persuasive arguments and listen to opposing views strengthens your leadership presence.*

- ❖ **Problem-Solving and Innovation:** *Creative solutions start with empathy and a willingness to explore new ideas.*
- ❖ **Emotional Intelligence:** *Understanding and managing emotions helps build trust and strong relationships.*
- ❖ **Team Collaboration:** *The best leaders bring people together, fostering mutual respect and accountability.*
- ❖ **Adaptability:** *Being open to change and staying calm under pressure sets leaders apart.*
- ❖ **Ethical Responsibility:** *Future leaders will be judged not only by what they achieve but how they achieve it.*

A Roadmap for Continuous Growth

Leadership isn't a "one-and-done" skill—it's something you develop through practice, reflection, and learning. Here's a step-by-step roadmap to guide you:

Step 1: Set Leadership Goals

Think about the areas where you want to grow. Do you want to become a better speaker? Improve your time management? Lead a community project? Write down your goals and be specific.

Example: Instead of writing, "I want to improve my public speaking," write, "I will practice delivering one speech per month and get feedback from a teacher or mentor."

Step 2: Build a Daily Leadership Habit

Consistency is key. Find small ways to practice leadership every day, whether it's volunteering for a new role in a group project, mentoring a younger student, or speaking up in discussions.

Step 3: Reflect and Adjust

At the end of each week, ask yourself:

- What went well?
- What could I improve?
- What did I learn about myself as a leader?

Reflection helps you celebrate wins and learn from challenges.

Step 4: Seek Mentors and Role Models

Great leaders don't grow in isolation. Surround yourself with mentors, teachers, and peers who inspire you. Learn from their stories and seek advice when you need it.

Step 5: Stay Adaptable

Remember that your goals may change as you grow—and that's okay. Adaptability is a sign of strength, not weakness.

Setting Long-Term Leadership Goals

Think about where you want to be in 5, 10, or even 20 years. Don't worry if you don't have every detail figured out yet—your vision will evolve over time. But having a sense of direction can help you stay motivated and focused.

Goal-Setting Tip: Break big goals into smaller steps. If your long-term goal is to become a leader in your field, start by taking on leadership roles in school, then community projects, and eventually internships or research opportunities.

Staying Adaptable and Resilient

The world is changing fast, and challenges are inevitable. Resilience doesn't mean avoiding failure—it means bouncing back stronger. When things don't go as planned, ask yourself:

1. What can I learn from this?
2. What's one step I can take to move forward?

Remember that every setback is an opportunity to grow.

Action Plan: Your Leadership Journal

Here's how to put everything you've learned into action:

1. **Start a Leadership Journal:** Write down your goals, successes, and lessons learned each week.
2. **Track Your Progress:** Look back every month to see how much you've grown.
3. **Celebrate Wins:** No matter how small, every step forward is worth celebrating.

Inspirational Final Words

Leadership isn't about being perfect—it's about showing up, learning, and making a positive impact. You don't need a title or a formal role to make a difference. Whether you're leading a classroom discussion, organizing a fundraiser, or supporting a friend, you're already a leader.

So, ask yourself: *What will I do today to lead with purpose?*

The future is yours to shape, and the world is waiting for leaders like you—leaders who listen, who create, who care, and who inspire. You've already taken the first step by reading this book. Now, go out there and lead with confidence, compassion, and courage.

SUPPLEMENTARY MATERIALS: TOOLS TO EMPOWER YOUR LEADERSHIP JOURNEY

In this section, you'll find practical tools to help you apply everything you've learned. Whether you're preparing for a speech, setting goals, or reflecting on your progress, these resources are here to guide you every step of the way.

Leadership Goal-Setting Template

Use this template to set clear, actionable goals.

Goal-Setting Worksheet:

- **Long-Term Goal:** What do you want to achieve in the next 1–5 years?
- **Short-Term Steps:** What small actions will help you reach your goal?
    - Step 1:
    - Step 2:
    - Step 3:
- **Challenges:** What obstacles might you face? How will you overcome them?
- **Accountability Partner:** Who will help you stay on track and give feedback?
- **Check-In Date:** When will you review your progress?

Speech and Debate Preparation Checklist

Use this checklist before delivering a speech or participating in a debate.

Before the Event:

- Research your topic thoroughly.
- Write a clear outline with an engaging introduction, main points, and conclusion.
- Add a personal story or example to make your message memorable.
- Practice out loud at least three times.

Day of the Event:

- Take deep breaths to calm nerves.
- Maintain eye contact with your audience.
- Pause for effect—don't rush your words.
- Be prepared for questions and feedback.

Problem-Solving Framework: Design Thinking Guide

This framework will guide you through the steps of creative problem-solving.

Empathy Phase:

- Who is impacted by the problem?
- How do they experience it?
- What emotions are involved?

Define Phase:

- What's the root cause of the issue?
- How can you clearly define the problem?

Ideation Phase:

- Brainstorm at least five potential solutions.
- Don't worry about whether ideas are realistic at first—just let creativity flow.

Prototype Phase:

- Choose one idea to test.
- Create a simple version of your solution (a draft, sketch, or outline).

Test Phase:

- Share your prototype with others and gather feedback.
- What worked? What didn't?

Time Management Planner

This planner will help you balance schoolwork, extracurriculars, and personal time.

Daily Planner:

- Morning: Top 3 priorities for the day
- Afternoon: Key tasks and deadlines
- Evening: Reflection (What went well today? What can I improve tomorrow?)

Weekly Planner:

- **Monday–Friday:** Assign study blocks and time for projects.
- **Weekend:** Include time for rest, hobbies, and any catch-up tasks.

Reflection Prompts for Journaling

Use these prompts to reflect on your growth as a leader:

1. What leadership skill did I practice this week?
2. What challenges did I face, and how did I respond?
3. Who inspired me, and what can I learn from them?
4. How did I make a positive impact today?
5. What's one thing I can do differently next week to improve?

Final Note on Tools and Growth

These tools aren't just checklists—they're steppingstones to becoming the best version of yourself. Leadership is a journey, not a destination, and every small step you take brings you closer to your goals.

CLOSING NOTE

As you finish this book, I hope you've discovered that leadership is not about perfection—it's about progress. It's about being brave enough to step forward, even when the path ahead isn't fully clear. Whether you're giving a speech, leading a team project, or helping someone who feels unseen, every small act of leadership matters.

Leadership starts within. It's how you choose to respond to challenges, how you lift others up, and how you carry yourself when no one is watching. It's not about waiting for the perfect moment—it's about creating the moment.

As you move forward, remember: you already have everything you need to make a difference. Your ideas, your values, your voice—they're powerful tools that can shape not only your life but the world around you.

Take the lessons from this book and make them your own. Start with small, intentional steps—embrace curiosity, practice empathy, and take pride in the leader you're becoming.

I'll leave you with this final thought: leadership isn't a destination—it's a lifelong journey. And while that journey will have ups and downs, the fact that you've made it this far tells me you're already on your way.

The future is waiting for your unique contributions. Go out there, lead with heart, and create a legacy that makes you proud.

Thank you for letting me be a part of your journey.

All the best,

Sumit Sharma

ABOUT THE AUTHOR

Sumit Sharma's leadership journey is one of resilience, innovation, and service. From leading teams across industries to empowering students to find their voice, Sumit has spent his life turning challenges into opportunities for growth.

In the early years of his career, Sumit served as the Captain of large commercial ships, leading diverse crews through unpredictable voyages and high-pressure situations. In this role, he learned that leadership isn't just about authority—it's about instilling trust, inspiring discipline, and making decisions that balance logic with empathy. He took these lessons from the open seas into the corporate world, where he excelled in leadership roles.

Sumit went on to become Head of Process Engineering for a Fortune 500 company in the supply chain industry, leading multiple teams and motivating them to excel under tight deadlines. His ability to foster collaboration and keep his teams focused earned him recognition for driving impactful, lasting results. His expertise in process improvement as a Master Black Belt (MBB) in Six Sigma, combined with his certifications as a Stanford Certified Project Manager (SCPM) and Certified Healthcare Financial Professional (CHFP), laid the foundation for his success as a strategic leader.

Currently serving as a senior executive in the healthcare industry, Sumit spearheads initiatives that improve care for thousands of patients while ensuring operational excellence. His leadership philosophy is rooted in the belief that discipline, empathy, and vision create stronger, more resilient teams. His commitment to excellence was recognized with the Phoenix HFMA Award for his contributions to healthcare innovation.

Sumit's passion for leadership extends far beyond the workplace. For over five years, he has dedicated his time to pro bono mentoring of high school students, teaching them public speaking, debate, and design thinking. Many of the students he mentored initially struggled with confidence, hesitant to speak up in front of others. Through his guidance, they not only mastered the art of public speaking and persuasive argument but also became leaders in their communities. Sumit believes that leadership must begin early in life and be reinforced with a sense of purpose and discipline—essential habits that empower young people to lead with confidence and character.

As a father of three, including two teenagers, Sumit is inspired daily by their resilience, curiosity, and ambition. This book was born from his desire to provide teenagers with the tools to discover their potential and shape the world around them.

"Empowering Tomorrow's Leaders: A Guide for Teens" is a reflection of Sumit's belief that leadership isn't defined by titles—it's defined by the ability to make a positive impact at every stage of life. His hope is that young leaders will read this book and find the courage to create change, face challenges head-on, and inspire others to do the same.

Sumit welcomes connections with readers, educators, and parents to discuss leadership development and mentorship. You can reach him for workshops, guidance, or speaking engagements at **sumitsharma1@live.com.**

Interested in a Future in Healthcare Leadership?

If you're passionate about leadership and curious about careers in healthcare, you may enjoy my other book, Transforming the Operating Room: Innovative Leadership Strategies for Surgical Efficiency. This book dives into the real-world challenges and leadership skills needed to improve surgical teams and hospital efficiency. Whether you aspire to be a doctor, nurse, administrator, or healthcare innovator, understanding healthcare leadership will give you a head start. Here is the link - https://a.co/d/0HAaoFy

www.ingramcontent.com/pod-product-compliance
Lightning Source LLC
Chambersburg PA
CBHW030822090426
42737CB00009B/838